CREATE YOUR LIFE

WITH GRACE AND EASE

Master the Rays of Experience
Create Harmony, Balance, and Opportunity

Michael G. Love

Practical Applications Book II

SPARK Publications
Charlotte, North Carolina

Create Your Life with Grace and Ease: Master the Rays of Experience (Practical Applications Book II)
Michael G. Love

Copyright © 2020 by Michael G. Love All rights reserved. No part of this book may be used or reproduced in any manner whatsoever without written permission from the author, except in the case of brief quotations embodied in critical articles or reviews. For permissions requests, please contact the author at mike@michaelglove.com.

Designed, produced, and published by SPARK Publications
SPARKpublications.com
Charlotte, North Carolina

Printed in the United States of America.
Softcover, August 2020, ISBN: 978-1-943070-92-3
E-book, August 2020, ISBN: 978-1-943070-93-0

CONTENTS

Introduction...5

CHAPTER 1
The Rays of Experience (Also Known as the Rays of Attributes) 13

CHAPTER 2
Harmony..17

CHAPTER 3
The Fourth Ray – Harmony through Conflict 23

CHAPTER 4
The Fifth Ray – Concrete Knowledge 33

CHAPTER 5
The Sixth Ray – Devotion and Idealism........................... 43

CHAPTER 6
Ritual and Ceremony 55

CHAPTER 7
The Seventh Ray – The Violet Flame of Saint Germain................ 59

CHAPTER 8
Separation and Connection....................................... 69

CHAPTER 9
The Seventh Ray – Gateway into Awareness 73

CHAPTER 10
You Are More..81

About the Artists 83

"It is time for you to choose your own condition; whether that be suffering and pain or joy and love, to draw the Spirit—the God of You—into this physical vessel, to know of the duality in your relative environment and to overcome, to choose the highest state of life within this environment, for Earth to choose to survive, or to live, to live as a spiritual being.

You have suffered. Is it not time for you to integrate, to be what you have never been on this planet before, and to feel the joy and the opportunity that no other environment offers before it is destroyed by your own suffering?"

– The Team

INTRODUCTION

Pain and suffering. I've had enough of it. How about you? Who said we have to live this way? Where is it written that life has to be experienced this way?

Many of us have experienced pain and suffering in our lifetimes. Who hasn't heard the expression "no pain, no gain"? What if it doesn't have to continue on this way? What if you could live your life with grace and ease? Would that be of interest to you?

If you are truly interested in experiencing a life of grace and ease, then you must change how you live your life. You must take charge of your life and change your beliefs about yourself and the world around you. Are you ready to do that, or would you rather continue on with the way things have been going?

If you are really serious about letting go of the old way of living with pain and suffering, use your imagination and envision what your life would be like when you create it with grace and ease. And then consider the process of how that becomes possible. It is not likely to occur overnight. You will need to work at it. And you will need some new techniques. The Rays are presented as a group of techniques to get you headed in the right direction. You can become a master of creating your life with grace and ease.

Change is one of the most discussed and written-about topics. Some people embrace change openly and encourage it. They believe that change is good. However, many of us, myself included, often find change to be uncomfortable. We would rather maintain the status quo but know that some change is necessary and accept it begrudgingly. A stubborn few resist change with all their might.

Change most always leads to something better. This is the message of the Twelve Rays: there is something better, much better in fact.

How do you change your life? You start with your thoughts. Only one individual on this planet is in charge of your thoughts: you. Where do your thoughts come from? They come from your beliefs about yourself and the world. How did your beliefs become yours? Through your individual life experiences.

Are you interested in changing your beliefs? Would you like to change the belief "I'm not _____ enough" to something different? If the answer is yes, then it's time to change what you are doing. Some people will tell you that change is hard. My experience is that any belief can be changed with the proper level of motivation.

Motivation is easily generated once you say to yourself, "I have had enough pain and suffering." We were never meant to suffer. Suffering is a bad habit, and like all habituated patterns, it can be changed to something new like grace and ease. Are you ready to let go of the bad habit of suffering?

Farmers used to plow their fields with a horse or ox, depending on where they lived, and used a simple, single plow made of metal. We have all seen this depicted in the movies. Then a new tool was invented and became available to farmers: a tractor. It was a game changer. Farmers became more efficient. They could tend to larger fields and farms, which resulted in greater crop yields and greater prosperity. In addition, tractors are multipurpose machines that can do far more than just plow fields. With the wide array of farm equipment that they can connect to, they make life easier for most farmers.

The Twelve Rays are tools that allow each and every one of us to become more efficient at life. They allow us to convert our lives from the old ways, which included pain and suffering, to the new ways, which deliver our earthly experiences with grace and ease. The Rays help us to open to new understandings of who we really are and why we are here at this time on this planet. They help us to direct our life experiences rather than just letting life happen around us. They help us to create goals for ourselves and achieve them.

The Twelve Rays are waiting for you to discover them. You can continue to live your life the way you have been, and that is perfectly fine. No one will fault you for continuing your established patterns. But if you long for something more in your life, then some changes are necessary.

The Rays are offered as tools to help you change. You are more than you think you are. No matter who or what you think you are, you are more than that. I hope you are open to expanding the limiting beliefs you hold about who you are and what you can achieve.

Throughout this workbook, and through all the works that I have published about the Twelve Rays, you will find quotes from sessions with the Team. The Team consists of a group of guides and teachers who communicate through the trance medium whom I will refer to as Julie. It is not her real name. We have been communicating with them in formal sessions since around 2005.

All the information we have about the Twelve Rays has been given to us by the Team. We know their names and could share them with you, but we have chosen not to. Humans love to give labels to things, and any name we would give you would be limiting in nature. Instead, we ask you to read the messages and feel the energy in their words. Judge for yourself if their words have integrity. You decide if the messages resonate with you or not.

Here is a short excerpt from a session where they talk about the Rays in general.

> *All these energies that we have spoken about flow through you. Becoming aware of them is simply a way to raise that consciousness to enlighten you to the power that you work with, that you avail yourself of. You choose every moment the energies that you bring to your being and by so doing you affect the energies of everything in your reality.*

The Rays flow through you even when you are unaware of them. When you decide to embrace the Rays and work with them, you embark upon a journey of change and personal expansion.

Are you ready to leave the horse and plow behind? Remember, that was hard, back breaking work. Are you ready to learn how to operate the tractor? Are you ready to learn how to create with grace and ease? The choice is yours!

If you are really serious about letting go of the old way of living with pain and suffering, use your imagination and envision what your life would be like when you create it with grace and ease. And then consider the process of how that becomes possible. It is not likely to occur overnight. You will need to work at it. And you will need some new tools, some new techniques. The Rays are presented as a new tool with a rich assortment of techniques to get you headed in the right direction. You can become a master of creating your life with grace and ease.

The Violet Flame of Saint Germain

This workbook focuses on the middle Rays, Rays Four through Seven. They are known as the Rays of Attributes or the Rays of Experience. One of these Rays is already known to many—the Seventh Ray, which is also known as the Violet Flame.

Most who have already heard of the Violet Flame associate it with the ascended master Saint Germain. I don't know how many people would associate the Violet Flame with the Seventh Ray. They are indeed one and the same. The Seventh Ray is the Violet Flame.

One of the first to write about the Violet Flame was Guy Ballard, using the pen name of Godfre Ray King. He founded the "I AM" movement to promote the teachings of Saint Germain. The teachings of Saint Germain were later expanded on by Mark and Marie Clare Prophet. They developed Violet Flame decrees and instructed their followers to begin reciting an individual decree three or nine times, increasing gradually. They suggest that, eventually, 144 repetitions would be appropriate.

The rosary comes to mind. The Catholic church is known for its rituals. As a recovering Catholic, I view the decree repetitions in the same manner as the repetitive prayers we were taught to say in my youth. I am not fond of those rituals, but others are very comfortable with it. That's fine. To each their own.

The Team has made a point of asserting that rituals inhibit personal growth. When Julie and I first heard this, it rather surprised us. But when you think about it, it does make sense. Rituals keep individuals stuck in certain belief loops. The Team has encouraged us to question dogma and not to engage in rituals, since the rituals only support the dogma.

What you will find in this workbook should not be viewed as rituals. I refer to them as guided journeys, and they should be used as guidelines to working with the Rays. Work with the guided journeys that are provided and make them your own. Embellish and personalize them. They are meant to be skeletons that you flesh out. Be creative with them, for creativity is the root of discovery and growth.

The Twelve Rays

The Twelve Rays are a modern metaphor for energies that have been emphasized in many eastern spiritual practices like Tai Chi, Qigong, and yoga. I believe that the Rays are easy for the Western mind to understand. In the twenty-first century, concepts like energy, matter, time, and space are all commonplace. The Rays are a modern metaphor for this life-force energy. The Rays are real. You can feel them. You can direct them. You can benefit from them. Here is a description of the Rays as energy from the Team.

> *From the heart of the Source emanates the Twelve Rays, and as these Rays lower in intensity through the dimensions, they create—as you are being created—light. This light is transmuted to liquid form moving down through the Microtrons [smallest form of consciousness energy], flowing into your physical being, flowing in through your pineal glands, into your nerves flowing through your nervous system, entering the blood through your veins.*
>
> *This light, it is the life force that carries the energy of who you are, your experience through this life and in between. It emanates out through your electronic body into your auric field. It flows through your brain cells. It sparks life in your muscles. It moves thought. It carries—it carries and communicates all these actions back to the Source. And it carries inharmonious action to be released back, to be cleansed, and to be evolved.*

The Twelve Rays are not associated with any ancient religious teachings. Nor are they associated with wellness systems like yoga, Reiki, acupuncture, or Ayurveda. The Twelve Rays represent a fresh, new metaphor for a concept that is thousands of years old.

These Rays are not visible to the human eye. They have no smell, no taste, but since they are energy, certain individuals can perceive them. You can train yourself to sense them. They exist all around us; they provide us with the tools we need to have these earthly experiences.

You don't have to be aware of these energies in order to survive here on Earth. Much like oxygen, which usually requires no active consideration from the individual, the Rays support us without our conscious interaction with them. However, since this energy contains consciousness, all the Rays respond to our conscious thoughts. They respond even when we are not consciously directing them. Our thoughts influence the energy of the Rays directly or indirectly.

As we move deeper into the digital age, concepts such as energy, wavelengths, particles, and quantum physics open mankind's awareness to new ways of thinking about the nature of reality. It seems that science is now actively considering consciousness as part of the theories they are developing to explain the results of their experiments. In a 2011 article in the *Journal of Cosmology* (vol. 14), Roger Penrose, PhD, and Stuart Hameroff, MD, wrote, "We conclude that consciousness plays an intrinsic role in the universe."

The Team mentions the Microtron in the above quote. You will notice that it is described as being the smallest form of conscious energy. Actually, the Team has indicated that all energy has consciousness. One of my favorite quotes from our sessions over the years is, "In order for consciousness to act, there must be consciousness to be acted upon." The first reference to consciousness is our conscious thoughts. The second reference is to the consciousness of the energy that is responding to our thoughts.

Having defined the Rays as a modern metaphor for life-force energy and more, I would like to point out that the Rays are easy to understand and even easier to benefit from. If you look at the diagram of the Rays, you will see that they are divided into three groups. The first group, the Rays of Aspect, are our Divine Heritage and are ours to use as children of the Creator in the various dimensions of creation, our physical dimension being one of those. But we use them in the other dimensions of creation also. The second group, the Rays of Attributes, are designed for our use in this physical dimension. They help us create our human experiences. The third group, the Rays of Soul Integration, which have only been available to us rather recently, bridge both this physical dimension and the other dimensions.

I have shared the information and the techniques about the Rays of Aspect in my book, *The Twelve Rays Practical Applications: Foundational Level Individual Workbook*. I refer to the Rays of Aspect as our Spiritual Heritage. As children of the Source, or All That Is, or whatever name you feel comfortable with, the Rays of Aspect are given to us as part of our Spiritual Lineage. We use the gifts that the first three Rays represent in all the dimensions that we find ourselves inhabiting. When we entered this dimension, we encountered forgetfulness. Many have lost track of their Spiritual Heritage.

I have published two workbooks that deal with the first three Rays. The first book, *The Twelve Rays: Practical Applications Foundational Level Individual Workbook*, is intended for individual use. The second workbook, *The Twelve Rays: Practical Applications Foundational Level Practitioner Workbook*, is intended for anyone who uses alternative healing modalities. Both workbooks have the same guided exercises in them. The difference between them is the intended audience. In the practitioner's guide, I take into consideration the other individual that the practitioner is working with.

The book you are now reading focuses on the second tier of Rays. In this book, you will learn techniques using the Rays of Attributes, Rays Four through

Seven. They are also referred to as the Rays of Experience. These Rays are very specific Rays intended for our use while here in this dimension, on this planet. The specific techniques that are included here will help you to:
- Create and express harmony in your life
- Balance your emotions
- Create and clarify personal goals and objectives
- Open yourself to the grander, greater expression of what you know yourself to be

Let me give you a quick overview of the Rays of Experience. The Fourth Ray is called Harmony through Conflict. Artists and musicians have a great deal of this energy. The two specific groups are mentioned because it is easy to understand how they are involved in self-expression through their art and music. Conflicts arise when their artistic creations don't perfectly capture their self-expression.

But aren't we all involved in self-expression in some fashion? Aren't the clothes that you wear part of your self-expression? The food you eat, the work you do, the friends you keep—aren't they all parts of your self-expression? And is anything more rife with conflict than relationships? This energy of the Fourth Ray interacts with the human emotions we experience when we encounter conflict. And as we work to resolve conflict, we strive to experience the emotion of harmony.

The Fifth Ray, Concrete Knowledge, helps us to discover and understand the scientific truths that are the foundation of our physical dimension. For example, it helps scientists deepen their understanding of our universe. Because it is a very mental energy, it can be used to balance those individuals who are very involved with their emotions.

The Sixth Ray is the Ray of Devotion and Idealism. Many groups of individuals have large amounts of this energy. I feel that perhaps the largest group is the clergy. It may seem like the ranks of the clergy may be shrinking in modern times. Not too long ago, every family was honored to have one of their own as a member of the clergy. When I was growing up, one of my aunts was a Grey Nun and one of my cousins was a Catholic priest.

Another group that I would include as having a great deal of this energy is the military. Even if you have not been involved with the military in this lifetime, I am certain you have experienced it in one of your other lifetimes. I believe this is also probably true for the clergy. If you are not comfortable with the concept of reincarnation, then just put that last comment aside for the time being. By protecting their homelands, soldiers demonstrate both devotion and idealism. They are so devoted that they are willing to risk everything to defend what they believe in. Of course, there are plenty of other occupations that show strong devotion and idealism.

The Fourth, Fifth, and Sixth Rays of Attributes (or Rays of Experience) enable us to have our unique human experiences. The Team refers to the Seventh Ray, the Violet Flame, as the Gateway into Awareness. Its purpose is to help us process our human experiences. We humans learn and grow though our personal experiences.

We continue to adjust our belief systems as a result of new experiences and their emotional impact on us. Think of the Seventh Ray as a process that allows us to integrate the lessons from past experience and resolve the residual emotional energy that is associated with them. It can help us expand our beliefs about who and what we are. This helps us to work more effectively with the new Rays, which are the Rays of Soul Integration and include Rays Eight through Twelve.

The Eighth Ray, or the Cleansing Ray, is technically part of the new Rays. We use it mostly in conjunction with the Seventh Ray. After working with the transmuting processes of the Seventh Ray, we use the Eighth Ray to replenish and balance personal energy. You can see why it goes nicely with the Seventh Ray.

The new Rays will be discussed in an upcoming book on their practical applications. The primary practical applications of these new Rays help us establish contact with our whole selves and having done that, bring more of our whole selves into this dimension. We each do that by connecting with our individual Body of Light. We can then begin to anchor our Body of Light into this physical dimension.

Maintaining a higher personal energetic level and anchoring more of our soul-level consciousness into our physical bodies enables us to begin to create a New Awareness here on this planet. This New Awareness is ours to create. Sounds very exciting, doesn't it?

That was a brief overview of the Twelve Rays. Let's dive a little more deeply in the Rays of Attributes as a group. Keep in mind that they are sub-Rays of the Third Ray, the Ray of Active Intelligence. The Third Ray is all about manifestation. I hope it makes sense to you that any energy used in our human experiences would be part of the overall concept of manifestation. The following chapter explains further.

"Do not skip over the Rays of Attributes or Rays of Experience, for it is these energies that the individual can use in your experience, in your life experience to raise yourself through the hardships you create, through the trials, through the challenges. And as you move to the higher energies, know that there is a progress."

– The Team

CHAPTER 1

The Rays of Experience

(Also Known as the Rays of Attributes)

Let me begin our discussion of the Rays of Experience with this excerpt from my book, *The Reality of Your Greatness: A Personal Journey through the Twelve Rays*.

> We all have various personality attributes that make us individuals. This creates a beautiful tapestry of personality traits that make each and every one of us unique. These attributes have been thoughtfully combined to provide the resources we need for our individual journeys in this dimension.
>
> It is easy to hold judgment about our individual attributes. Why am I this way, or why can't I be more like her or him? My sister got all the good looks in the family, while I did well in school. I'm just a plain Jane. It's not fair. My brother is a natural-born athlete. He was good at any sport he played. My little sister is a rebel. She is the artist. Mom and Dad let her get away with everything. My brother Joey is a born salesman. He can sell ice to Eskimos. The judgments go on and on.
>
> It is easy to judge when we forget what our souls' plans are. We come to this dimension with intention. We are not just dropped off at a summer camp, 'See you in two weeks. Have fun.' A great deal of planning goes into each and every incarnation. Human personality traits are a very important part of that planning, and as we will soon see, the

Rays of Attributes help reinforce those individual character traits. Here is the first introduction to the Rays of Attributes from the Team.

> *We last spoke of the Third Ray, the Ray of Active Intelligence. Through this Ray, Earth's lessons are learned, and the Creator experiences through the cosmic plan. Through this Ray, traveling through from Source to your planet, flow the Fourth, the Fifth, the Sixth, and the Seventh Rays.*
>
> *Rays Four through, particularly through, Six, let us exclude Ray Seven for a moment, these are Rays of Attributes. Each of you accesses varying amounts of the energies in these Rays depending on what you are experiencing, your personality, your mission, the plan, when you were called upon. Fear not in using them, but use them in their highest potential, in the clearest, highest vibration of each. Use them delicately. Use them with the wisdom, the love, the intelligence, and the will provided through the first three Rays.*
>
> *Each individual has a little bit of each of these Rays. Some, depending on their talents and personalities, draw through them more of one than the other.*

The Rays of Attributes, or as they are sometimes called, the Rays of Experience, are specifically designed for our use here in this dimension. The first three Rays, the Rays of Aspect that are covered in the foundational workbook, are part of our Divine Heritage. We use them in all the dimensions of our existence, which includes this Earth dimension.

I have presented the Rays of Experience in sequential order because that is how we received them. However, since each of us has various amounts of these Rays at any given time, you can use any one of these in any sequence you choose. The notable exception is the Seventh Ray. I suggest using the Seventh Ray in combination with the Eighth Ray. I'll explain more about that in the chapter on the Seventh Ray.

The same is pretty much true for the first three Rays. You can use them individually anytime you wish. In the foundational workbook, I have given some specific exercises that use the First and the Third Rays together. But generally speaking, the first three Rays are fine to use individually.

Here is an additional comment the Team gave about the Rays of Attributes.

> *Do not skip over the Rays of Attributes or Rays of Experience, for it is these energies that the individual can use in your experience, in your life experience to raise yourself through the hardships you create, through the trials, through the challenges. And as you move to the higher energies know that there is a progress.*

Keep in mind that we come here to this dimension in order to experience life here. It is through these life experiences that our souls, or whole selves, experience growth. We take these experiences back with us when we leave this dimension and integrate them into our whole selves, which is where all our experiences in all the dimensions are aggregated and integrated.

We use color, music, and words in the things that we create to express ourselves. What we are expressing is some personal insight that we choose to share with others. One form of harmony, then, has to do with perfecting that personal expression that we are sharing.

CHAPTER 2

Harmony

When I think of the meaning of harmony, I immediately think of music. That is most likely because I have played a guitar for over fifty years. Even if you don't play a musical instrument, I would bet that you too most likely think of music when you see the word harmony. Let's start with music then.

Each note resonates at a certain vibrational frequency. Middle C vibrates at around 262 hertz. This means that it vibrates at 262 times per second. The note G vibrates at 392 hertz. When you play them both together, they create harmony. Once you add in an E note at about 330 hertz and play them altogether, you have a fundamental construct of music, a musical chord. In this case, a C chord. I'm sure there is some mathematical formula here somewhere, but I'm going to stop the music lesson here.

The point is, when certain notes are played together, they sound most pleasing, and when certain other notes are played together, they are very irritating. Some forms of music, most notably jazz music, are oftentimes meant to be discordant. Not that the jazz musicians are intending to be annoying, but they use music to create a different sound, a more unique expression of the regular scales. This is just one of the factors that differentiates jazz from other forms of music.

Keep in mind that the brain interprets what is harmonic, and it is usually based on the commonly accepted definitions of harmony that society holds. Think about music around the world. Some cultures value music that people in the West find positively irritating. And vice versa of course. So we are not dealing with absolutes here, but rather what is commonly accepted.

Music evokes emotions from us when the notes are composed in certain patterns over time. We generally refer to this as a song. We can add words to the music to tell a story that further identifies the emotions that are associated with the song. The notes and the composition along with the rhythm and the words all combine to create a finished work of art.

Consider color for a moment. There is clearly harmony in color. We find some colors complement each other very well, and others contrast. The primary colors are red, blue, and yellow. Their complementary colors are made of equal parts of the other two colors mixed. The complement of red is green, which is a one-to-one mixture of yellow and blue. Yellow's complement is purple, which is made of red and blue. And blue's complement is orange, a mix of yellow and red. Our brains seem to find complementary colors to be pleasing.

Now, certain other colors clash. I think there is some cultural influence involved with colors, but probably less than with music. The brain finds some color combinations more harmonic than others.

When you view a painting, you probably first notice the images in the picture. Some paintings are clear representations of images that are well known to us, such as people, buildings, landscapes, and other images that we might find anywhere. Other paintings are more abstract, and here the use of color is likely more important than the use of shapes. Sometimes the images in the painting tell the story along with the color, and other times the colors tell the primary story with the more abstract images filling in the rest of the story. I'm not trying to turn this into a conversation about art appreciation. I just want to get you to think about harmony.

Let me remind you that the first three Rays are represented with the colors red, blue, and yellow respectively. The Rays of Attributes are represented with the complementary colors of green, orange, and violet.

We use color, music, and words in the things that we create to express ourselves. What we are expressing is some personal insight that we choose to share with others. One form of harmony, then, has to do with perfecting that personal expression that we are sharing. Let's refer to that as harmony of expression. Other types of harmonies have to do with our personal experiences. Let's refer to them as harmonies of experience.

What are examples of harmony of experience? How about relationships? Think of all the different types of relationships we have with others. We have our family members, siblings, and parents. Then, when we get older, we very likely have a significant other and perhaps children of our own. There is the extended family of aunts and uncles, cousins, nephews, and nieces. We have our friends, neighbors, and the individuals we work with. The list can go on and on. Trying to maintain harmony in all of these relationships can be a full-time job.

There is one relationship, however, that I haven't mentioned. That is the relationship we have with ourselves. And this might possibly be the most difficult relationship of them all. How do we keep the relationship we have with ourselves harmonious? Many individuals seem to be their own worst critic. They seem to have some expectations about life that they find difficult to achieve.

Unrealistic expectations of achievement or behavior may prevent them from ever having a good relationship with themselves.

Hopefully, our relationship with ourselves improves over time. The more we figure out who we are, the more we understand what is reasonable and what is not, the easier it gets to create that personal harmonious relationship.

The same holds true for the other relationships mentioned above. The more we understand who we are and why we are here, the more harmonious those relationships become. When we understand that everyone comes into this life experience with intention, and we don't know what that might be for others, it becomes easier to lose judgment about what others are doing with their lives. It becomes easier to offer our friends compassion when they need it, rather than judgment. It becomes easier to love them when we can see beyond the current masks that they are wearing and know that they are children of the Creator just as we are. All of this leads to more harmonious relationships.

Our relationships with ourselves include our relationships with our physical bodies. A cursory look at the health-care industry shows that we all could do a better job of maintaining harmony within our physical bodies. I'm sure most of us could lose a little weight, get a little more exercise, eat a little better, and get the appropriate amount of sleep every night.

I find this entire concept of our relationships with our bodies to be fascinating. I love to encourage discussion about it. Individuals have so many different points of view about the subject. We will return to this topic when we discuss the Seventh Ray.

The relationships we have with ourselves involve more than just our physical bodies because we simultaneously exist beyond this physical dimension. The Rays of Experience support us in our experience of this earthly dimension. There are other Rays that support our connections to those aspects of ourselves that are beyond this dimension. One of these aspects is often referred to as one's higher self. I prefer referring to it as one's whole self.

We use the new, higher Rays to remind us of our connections to our whole selves. And the promise of these new Rays is to actually bring more of our higher selves into this dimension. The Tenth Ray is called the Body of Light, and we can begin to use this Ray to anchor into this physical dimension, to anchor into our physical bodies, that part of our whole selves that we refer to as the Body of Light. The process of how to do that is in the third workbook of this series. I highly recommend spending the time to become familiar with the Rays of Experience before moving forward with the higher Rays.

This leaves one remaining relationship to briefly discuss. And that is our relationship with the Creator. Since we are all children of the Creator, we are connected to and part of the Creator in ways that are difficult for our physical minds to comprehend. When we work with the Rays of Aspect, Rays One through Three, we are embracing that relationship. We are embracing our Divine Heritage. If you have not worked with the Rays of Aspect, I strongly recommend that you take the time to open yourself to your Divine Heritage that the first three Rays represent. You can learn more about them in the first workbook of this series entitled *The Twelve Rays: Practical Applications. Foundational Level Individual Workbook.*

The idea of harmony is very important when it comes to the Rays of Experience. This brief treatment of it should help us when we get to learn about the individual Rays.

I want to share one more concept with you about the Rays. During one of our sessions, the Team mentioned how they perceive the Rays. Here is what they had to say.

> *You wonder about the Rays. We hear you ask how to use the Rays, the Fourth, the Fifth, and the Sixth. They are vibrations. We see them as color. We hear them as notes. We feel them as thought. There are many applications for their use. You live inside the vibrations and the tools of knowledge allow you to consciously access these vibrations.*

As we move through the Rays of Experience, I will share with you the colors that the individual Rays represent through beautiful, original artwork created by Melinda Radcliffe. I find this artwork to be very impressionistic and think that is a good way to represent the Rays. Some shapes and images in them are recognizable, but they are mostly open to individual insight and experience. Each individual Ray is very robust and has a broad energetic bandwidth. This means each can be experienced from very different perspectives.

I will also share original music composed and performed by Richard Shulman. He created a unique track of music for each Ray. As long as I have known Richard, he has been creating musical soul portraits for individuals. He has the ability to tune into an individual's energy and play the music that he hears. I asked him if he could tune into me while I tuned into a specific Ray, and this music is the result of those sessions.

Feel free to work with the artwork or the music individually. When you are ready, work with them together for a different experience. I have combined them for each Ray for your individual use on my YouTube channel. The specific file is indicated in each of the upcoming chapters.

I also provide the description, or thought, that the Team gave for each of the Rays. Each Ray chapter has an exercise meant to help you connect with the energy of that Ray. The "Listen, Feel, and Connect" sections are short exercises to bring these three aspects of each Ray—the color, the sound, and the concept—to life for you. I hope you take the time to benefit from them. I hope these exercises help you to tune into the vibration of each Ray. Keep in mind that each Ray is energy, and all energy vibrates.

You will also find a guided journey in each Ray chapter that affords you a practical example of how to use the Rays. Think of these guided journeys as starting-out points. Once you feel comfortable with the journeys that are in this workbook, develop your own and use them in ways that benefit you personally.

Let's begin to work with the Rays of Attributes by starting with the Fourth Ray, the Ray of Harmony through Conflict.

CHAPTER 3

The Fourth Ray
Harmony through Conflict

"There is no way to avoid conflict as a human in your environment unless you place yourself in a comatose state. If you were to go and sit on a mountain you could not escape conflict, for your mind would begin to wander to the valley below."

– The Team

The word "conflict" is a common antonym of the word "harmony." I want to talk about three different types of conflict—natural, mental, and emotional. Natural conflict is the type of conflict that we see in the physical world. Think of opposites, like hot and cold. Mental conflicts have to do with the beliefs we hold about ourselves and the world around us. They create conflicts because they are illusions. Emotional conflicts are illusions also. These are based in our feelings about ourselves and the rest of the world.

You have probably heard the statement that we live in a reality of duality. To me, that means that we live in a world of opposites. These are what I refer to as natural conflicts. Examples are everywhere you look. Male and female, light and dark, hot and cold—these are just a few to consider. The list goes on and on. It is possible for many of us to experience both aspects of the duality.

If you consider them more closely, they are really extremes of something else. Hot and cold are extremes of temperature. Bright and dark are really extremes of light. Male and female, well you get the point. We really don't fully appreciate the one extreme without experiencing the other. If it were bright all the time, it would be hard to experience dark. When we have the opportunity to experience both, we then come to a greater understanding of each and find a synthesis of the two. This creates harmony. This is another example of harmony through experience.

Mental conflicts are plentiful. These are beliefs that are really illusions. For example, if you believe you are not good enough, then you will experience all kinds of conflicts in your life because that belief simply isn't true. So you work at understanding and expressing your true value as a human being and as a child of the Creator. Then you can change your belief that you are not good enough and eliminate all the conflict associated with it.

We also have emotional conflicts. The opposite of love is considered by many to be fear. Compassion may be the opposite of apathy, generosity the opposite of greed, and so on. We get to experience as many of these oppositions as we choose. Often, the pursuit of these experiences leads to specific life experiences. You may choose a career where you can be totally indifferent to others, believe the end justifies the means, or select a path that allows you to experience compassion through service to others. Or perhaps experience both! When we understand the apathy of the narcissist and the compassion of the individual in service to others, then we have a better understanding of what the self is.

We come into this dimension to have these experiences. And while this may seem like an awful lot of conflict, it does indeed lead to harmony. This Fourth Ray, Harmony through Conflict, is very helpful as we discover varied experiences here on Earth. As we experience duality in our lives, we often share our insights through self-expression. Some individuals have careers that are totally about self-expression. Think of painters, sculptors, musicians, and dancers. What they create are their personal interpretations of their experiences.

The Team introduced the Fourth Ray this way.

> *The Fourth Ray can be called Harmony through Conflict. And most [who] experience this Ray first experience the conflict; then through raising up the vibration, they can move into harmony. We associate a vibrational color of green to this Ray energy. And you find that most artists and musicians hold a great deal of this energy. They experience both outer and inner conflict. They wrestle with this as they create and struggle to find that harmonious place.*

You can see that they mentioned artists and musicians specifically. I am sure they did not mean to exclude others. They were just using these two groups as perhaps obvious examples. I like to include anyone who is engaged in self-expression. So my list is a lot longer. It also includes writers.

Think of all the ways you express yourself at home: your furniture, your color schemes, even the food you prepare. And if you work outside of your home, think about your self-expression at your workplace. And of course, there are other locations and opportunities for self-expression. Even our choices for recreation are a form of self-expression.

Imagination

If you are involved in self-expression—and really who isn't?—a good imagination is a valuable asset. Like most things, the more you use your imagination, the better you get at it. Most of us were pretty good at using our imaginations when we were younger. But many seem to have less and less opportunity to practice using their imaginations as they get older. So our first exercise in working with the Fourth Ray is a fun exercise that uses your imagination.

Listen, Feel, and Connect Exercise 1:
THE FOURTH RAY

This exercise will take about ten minutes, and all you have to do is listen, feel, and connect. In this first exercise, focus your attention on the painting of the Fourth Ray pictured here. At the same time, listen to the music of the Fourth Ray if you have the CD. Alternatively, I created a video that has the painting and the music together. Visit my website, thetwelverays.com, to play the video. Let me suggest that you also have paper and something to write with.

Now, all you need to do is stay in the moment. Don't think about what you did last evening. Don't think about what you are going to do tomorrow. Just stay in the present moment and let the music and the painting help you to connect to the energy of the Fourth Ray. Allow them to help the Fourth Ray come alive for you.

It is very likely that you will gain some interesting insights when you finish with the exercise. And just like those vivid dreams you have just before you wake in the morning, they quickly fade away. So the faster you can capture them on paper the more complete they will be for you.

Now a quick word about skipping over the exercises. I know it is easy to skip over the exercises and keep on reading. But if you do that, you won't get the same level of understanding out of the discussion that follows the exercise. It is all up to you to decide whether you want to invest that ten minutes for this exercise. When you are ready to proceed, find a place where you can comfortably sit uninterrupted. Make sure you are holding nothing but the picture of the Fourth Ray.

Start the music and allow yourself to focus on the painting. Use your imagination. Go ahead and start the exercise now.

Welcome back. Remember to capture your insights as quickly as you can. What did you see in the picture? I'm willing to bet that you saw more than you thought you would see. What images came to life for you? And how did the music complement your experience? Did you find it soothing and calming, or was it agitating and disruptive? Take a minute or two to think about these questions. Write down any insights that you get.

These exercises are intended to help you to connect with the energy and the concept of the particular Ray you are working with; there is no specific goal in mind other than that. The upcoming guided journeys will have more specific goals. The exercises are just a basic introduction to the Ray. Remember, the Team said they hear them as notes, see them as colors, and feel them as thoughts. That is what the goals of the exercises are—to hear, see, feel, and connect with each individual Ray.

 ## Guided Journey 1: THE FOURTH RAY

All of us have varying levels of the Rays of Experience, as we have discussed above. Within that framework, there is also a variance depending on what you are currently focused on. So if you are an artist of some sort, but you are driving your kids to school in the morning, you currently have a different amount of this energy than if you were in the middle of creating something. The same goes for the other Rays of Experience.

Each of these Rays of Experience can be used on demand, so to speak. You can intentionally ramp them up. And that is what we will do now—increase your amount of Fourth Ray energy—and we will do so for a specific purpose. This guided journey is for anyone who is attempting to create something like a painting, sculpture, song, or poem that represents a concept they are attempting to share with the rest of us. So we are looking for the best way to express that insight. The harmony that we are seeking is harmony of expression.

Make sure you have paper and pen handy. Write down and finish the following sentence: I want to express how I feel about _____. For example, "I want to express how I feel about sunsets." Now take what you wrote in and write another sentence: _____ make(s) me feel _____.

To go with the previous example, "Sunsets make me feel calm." Now you know what you want to express and the feeling it gives you. In this guided journey, you'll find the best way for you to express yourself.

When you have completed the two sentences above, then begin the guided journey. Since this is a rather long guided journey, I suggest that you record yourself reading through the meditation after you've read it all the way first. Or visit my website, thetwelverays.com, and listen to my recording of it. When you are ready to proceed, find yourself a quiet place to sit comfortably where you won't be interrupted. I suggest having your feet firmly on the floor sitting upright. If you are more comfortable in another position, then by all means do what feels best. Concentrate on what it is you want to express and how it makes you feel.

This is the part that you will want to read through and either record on your own or listen to on the website. Have fun working with the Fourth Ray this way.

Let's begin this guided journey by taking a relaxing, gentle breath in, and then slowly breathe out. Take another relaxing breath in, breathing in fresh, relaxing air. When you exhale, let go of any tension or stress you may be feeling. One more gentle breath in, breathing in relaxing air, and gently exhale, releasing any stress or tension you may still be feeling. Very good.

Now imagine yourself comfortably seated in a darkened movie theater. You are all alone in this theater. Remember why you are here. "I want to express how I feel about _____." (Fill in your answer.) "I want to do this because it makes me feel _____."

Remember that the color of the Fourth Ray is green, and visualize the screen lighting up with a beautiful green color. And as the screen lights up, it begins to fill the entire room with beautiful green energy. You can gently breathe this energy in through your nose with each inhale. You can feel yourself totally surrounded by this energy.

Now state your intention once again and keep your eyes focused on the movie screen. Allow the images to appear. Remember that the images represent the feeling. If you don't start seeing images right away, simply restate your desire again.

If you don't see any images after a couple of minutes, listen. Do you hear anything? You may be hearing words or hearing music! Perhaps you are hearing sounds. Take a moment to sense if you hear anything.

If you are not getting any images or sounds, then check into how you feel. What are you currently feeling, and where are you feeling it? If you have a noticeable feeling in your body, what does that feeling remind you of, and why are you feeling it in that portion of your body?

Look for insights in the images, sounds, or feelings that you are receiving. If you feel that they are expressing what you are seeking to express, then great. If they are not quite what you think they should be, then communicate what is missing. Say to yourself, there should be a little more of this or not so much of that. Take a couple of minutes to get your best answer.

(Wait two minutes.)

I hope that you have the answers that you came here for. If you are still not sure, or haven't actually received anything, don't worry. You didn't do anything wrong. Like most new experiences, you will get better with practice. You can complete this guided journey as often as you wish, and each time, you will feel more and more comfortable with it.

Hopefully, you are filled with wonderful new insights and know exciting ways to express them. It is now time to return to your normal awakened state. Take a gentle breath in, and as you do begin to allow your consciousness to return to your physical body. Take another gentle breath in and gently wiggle your fingers and your toes, feeling your consciousness more fully returning.

Take one more gentle breath in and feel your arms and your legs. When you are ready, gently open your eyes and return to this place and time feeling relaxed, refreshed, and better than you have felt all day. Welcome back!

Now as quickly as you can, grab your pen and paper and capture all the wonderful insights that you received during this relaxing and refreshing exercise. Once you have everything written down you can start devising ways to create the objects that will best express your insights.

Balancing

Interestingly, the Rays of Experience can be used to help balance our energies. When we experience too much of a certain Ray, we can use a complementary Ray to help balance us. The Fourth Ray is a very emotional Ray. Too much of this Ray can easily put someone off balance. Here is how the Team describes this Ray.

> *Energies of this Fourth Ray tend to affect people in very emotional ways. Individuals [who] are experiencing this Ray tend to be very earthbound in their activities. They enjoy activities such as hiking, mountain climbing, horseback riding, working in the dirt, being with mother nature. And they tend to find, when in a situation of conflict, that they spin around and around, and then other emotions tend to go high and low, much like a roller coaster.*
>
> *They tend to live and focus a great amount of energy in their solar plexus, which is a very emotional chakra. And to balance them, they need to travel; they need to raise their energies higher into the mind. This creates a natural balance, to lift their energy from the solar plexus region. And they need to work on moving this energy of the Fourth Ray to a higher vibration and find this harmonious state.*

Without jumping too far ahead of ourselves, the Fifth Ray is often referred to as the Mental Ray. As you might imagine, this is a very good Ray to help balance individuals with high levels of the Fourth Ray. We will talk more about this in the next chapter. And in a likewise manner, individuals who are too much in their heads can find balance with this Fourth Ray.

CHAPTER 4

The Fifth Ray
Concrete Knowledge

"This is a very mental energy and is quite available on your planet as so many are living in their mental energies, sometimes stuck there. This energy is quite beneficial for those that are earthbound in their energies. It can be used quite effectively to balance and lift them when planted too firmly."

– The Team

Try to imagine what life was like one hundred years ago, in the early 1920s. People who had lived on farms their whole lives were moving to the city, mainly because that is where the jobs were, mostly in manufacturing. In my hometown of Buffalo, New York, you can still see the railroad tracks lined with old, empty factories that were the lifeblood of the residential communities. Workers could literally walk to their jobs in the factories. The men and women who worked in those factories worked hard, and they came home tired. There was a lot of manual labor.

The biggest churches in Buffalo are in these working-class communities. And, of course, the best food around was in the restaurants in these communities, which had very little ethnic diversity. Neighborhood parks where people could go and relax were also plentiful.

Television wasn't around yet. Moving pictures were the latest rage. The radio was something new, but there were very few stations available until later in the mid-1920s. No one had even dreamed of a computer or the Internet. The point I am trying to make is that there was not, generally speaking, a lot of mental activity used while at work. Manual work is hard and takes its toll on the body. And it wasn't just those individuals in the factories who were working hard. Plenty of people were still back on the farms, in the mines, on the docks, and elsewhere working just as hard, if not harder.

Move ahead fifty years to the 1970s, and more people were living in the suburbs due to the growing cities. More young people (us baby boomers) were going to college. It was the beginning of this new age of computers. My first job out of graduate school was as a computer programmer. When I arrived at work back then, I wasn't dressed in overalls. I had on a shirt and tie. I didn't work at a drill press, or a lathe, or on an assembly line. I turned on my CRT (as we called them back then), and then I worked in my head creating computer programs that would solve business problems. I came home tired but not physically exhausted. I came home mentally exhausted. I'm sure I had a lot of Fifth Ray energy at the time.

Now move ahead another fifty years to the early 2020s. I'm still typing this manuscript at my personal computer, but I'm not really thinking as in problem-solving. I'm thinking about how best to express the concepts I am sharing at the moment. It seems to me that I have more Fourth Ray energy these days.

The Mental Ray

The Fifth Ray is also known as the Mental Ray. Anytime you are engaged in heavy duty mental activity, you are calling on this energy. Of all the Rays, I believe this particular Ray is used in the widest range from low amounts to very high amounts. I mentioned in the proceeding chapter that low amounts of this Ray can be used to balance individuals who are too involved in their emotions. At the other end of the spectrum, this Ray is used by scientists who are able to conceptualize the mysteries of the universe. Most people these days work using their minds in some way, calling on the mid rage of this Ray. Here is how the Team described this Ray.

> *The Fifth Ray is an orange, an orange vibration, and it is known as the vibration and energy of pure intelligence, of concrete knowledge. The great scientists on your planet hold a great deal of this energy. The great concepts for your planet flow through this energy. Individuals in this energy are able to conceptualize; they are able to synthesize; they are able to take apart a concept and put it back together and see the purposeful meaning as it pertains to life on Earth. For those few individuals [who] can hold this vibration, these new concepts become available.*
>
> *As new principles come down through this Ray to your Earth, they are available in many locations to those individuals [who] have raised their vibration and can hold it at this level and accept the wisdom that flows.*
>
> *This is a very mental energy and is quite available on your planet as so many are living in their mental energies, sometimes stuck there. This energy is quite beneficial for those [who] are earthbound in their energies. It can be used quite effectively to balance and lift them when planted too firmly.*

It is no wonder that people in this digital age are living in their mental energy. The Team indicates that they are sometimes stuck there. This is where the Fourth Ray energy can help balance them. It is time once again to do a quick exercise to connect with the energy of the Fifth Ray.

Listen, Feel, and Connect Exercise 2:
THE FIFTH RAY

This exercise will take about ten minutes, and all you have to do is listen, feel, and connect. In this second exercise, focus your attention on the Fifth Ray painting pictured here while listening to the music of the Fifth Ray.

To prepare yourself for this exercise, have a copy of the painting in front of you along with the music. If you prefer, you can find a video of the painting and the music together on my YouTube channel. To view the video, visit my website, thetwelverays.com, for the link. Make sure you have paper and something to write with. It is very likely that you will get some interesting insights when you finish with the exercise. And just like those vivid dreams you have just before you wake in the morning, they quickly fade away. So the faster you can capture them on paper, the more complete they will be for you.

Remember, all you need to do is stay in the moment. Don't think about what you did last evening. Don't think about what you are going to do tomorrow.

Just stay in the present moment and let the music and the painting help you to connect to the energy of the Fifth Ray. Allow them to help the Mental Ray come alive for you. When you are ready to proceed, find a place where you can comfortably sit uninterrupted. Make sure you are holding the picture of the Fifth Ray.

Start the music and allow yourself to focus on the painting. Use your imagination. Go ahead and start the exercise now.

Welcome back. Remember to capture your insights as quickly as you can. What did you see in the picture? I'm willing to bet that you saw more than you thought you would see. What images came to life for you? And how did the music complement your experience? Did you find it soothing and calming or was it agitating and disruptive? Take a minute or two to think about these questions. Write down any insights you gain.

This exercise is intended to help you to connect with the energy and the concept of the Fifth Ray. We didn't have a specific goal in mind other than that. The upcoming guided journey will have more specific goals. This exercise is just a basic introduction to the Fifth Ray. Remember that the Team hear the Rays as notes, see them as colors, and feel them as thoughts. That is the goal of this exercise: to hear, see, feel, and connect with the Fifth Ray.

Guided Journey 2: THE FIFTH RAY

Around late August, most students are returning to school. If you are the parent of a freshman college student, you will experience some strong emotions as your child heads off to college for the first time. You might even get the opportunity to drop them off at their new dorm. It is hard to imagine it not being an emotional event. As you endure the endless drive back home, your teary-eyed teenager most likely has already moved on to the next thing, already back into their head with the many new things they need to focus on.

This is a great example of balancing. Sometimes this process occurs naturally, but other times, you have to actively restore your energetic balance. When you feel overwhelmed by your emotions, use this guided journey to help you create balance once again in your energetic field.

If you haven't had the experience of dropping your child off at college, perhaps you can remember back to their first day of school or perhaps dropping your child off at summer camp. Any memory of separation will work as long as you can feel the emotion.

Your intention here is to rebalance your energy. Connect with the energy of the Fifth Ray and bring it into your body to restore your balance. We will use a technique that allows you to step back, shift perspective, and see a bigger picture. And with this new understanding, your emotions will recalibrate and find balance.

Since this is a rather long guided journey, I suggest that you record yourself after reading it through all the way first. Or you can visit my website, thetwelverays.com, and listen to my recording of it. When you are ready to proceed, find yourself a quiet place to sit comfortably where you won't be interrupted. I suggest having your feet firmly on the floor sitting upright. If you are more comfortable in another position, then by all means do what feels best. Focus on the areas you feel are overwhelmed. Now let's begin.

Bring your attention to your breathing. Take a deep, gentle breath in. Allow yourself to relax with each inhale. Take another gentle breath in and, with every exhale, let go of any stress or tension you may be feeling. Good. Take one more gentle breath in, relaxing as you do, and then exhale, releasing any stress or tension you may still be feeling.

Think about the cause of the emotions you are feeling. Using our example of dropping your child off at college, take a step back and consider the bigger picture. This is not just about you. Think about what this means for your child. It is the beginning of a new chapter for them. How exciting!

Perhaps you are not old enough to have college children. Perhaps there is some other event like getting married or starting a new job that is the source of the emotions you are feeling. Use the same approach. Take a step back and look at the bigger picture. It is very likely that the emotions you are feeling are temporary in nature. Even if you currently see the event in some negative light, there is most likely a silver lining to that dark cloud.

Envision the orange energy of the Fifth Ray and bring it to you. Surround yourself with the energy and let it gently caress you. And as you feel it blending with your energy, feel the balance being restored. Direct this orange energy to your root chakra at the base of your spine. The energy of this chakra tends to focus on survival, food, shelter, and companionship. Bring this energy into this area and allow it to help balance the emotions you find there. Most problems turn out to be temporary learning opportunities. You have already learned a technique to get to the root of a problem by using the First Ray. And you know how to create a plan to move beyond it by using the Third Ray. Right now, we are interested in balancing your emotions with this mental energy.

Direct the orange energy now to your sacral chakra, which is located just below your navel. The energy of this chakra is all about relationships. Most relationship problems come from the illusion of separation. Use this energy to review your connections to those individual relationships that are causing distress. Allow yourself to step back and see the bigger picture. What do these relationships really mean to you? If they still have meaning in them, then renew your connection. If it is time to let them go, then do so in a loving manner. Renew or release, it is your choice.

Next, direct the energy of the Fifth Ray to your solar plexus. This is a very emotional chakra. This chakra has to do with personal power. Most people benefit greatly from balancing their third chakra energy. Many individuals suffer from self-esteem issues, thinking they're not (fill in the blank) enough. I'm not good enough, young enough, pretty enough, rich enough. You get the picture. Nobody is good at everything. Focus on what you are good at. We all have talents. Honor your talents and know that you can achieve almost anything you set your mind to. You can always improve areas where you feel improvement is necessary.

The next area for balancing is your heart chakra. Bring the orange energy into the middle of your chest and feel the balance restoring your emotions there. The heart chakra is, of course, the center of love. Too little love is not healthy. If you believe that you have too little love in your life, take a step back and look again at the big picture. Start with your relationship with yourself. You need to have a healthy relationship with yourself before you can have healthy relationships with others. If you believe your relationship with yourself could use some improvement, then use the First and Third Rays to make positive change.

We continue with the fifth chakra, which is located in your throat. The throat chakra is all about self-expression, speaking your truth. Bring the orange energy into this area to help you balance the energy here. You may feel that for some reason or another, it is a waste of time to try to express yourself. Again, take a look at the big picture and ask yourself if that is really true. Look around you and remember that everything you see started off as a thought in someone's mind. Your thoughts are just as important. Use the energy of the Fifth Ray to balance any emotions that are preventing you from sharing your thoughts with the rest of us.

The sixth chakra is the center for your intuitive abilities. This chakra is also referred to as the Third Eye. Many individuals place a high priority on opening their Third Eye, which can cause frustration. You may know others who are very intuitive. It is not required that you have your Third Eye open. Intuition increases as your overall energetic level increases. Focus on raising your overall energetic level, and your intuition will adjust accordingly. In the meantime, use this energy to maintain balance in this energy center.

The crown chakra represents our connection to the Divine. Some individuals are too worldly, while others are too spiritual. Use the energy of the Fifth Ray to help you create a balance between the two that is just right for you.

Now take a gentle breath in and envision a column of orange light above your head. Invite it to move down through your entire body, beyond the root chakra, flowing into your legs and down into your feet, and then to Mother Earth. Feel the balance in your entire body. Good.

In a moment we will begin our journey back. Take a minute and feel how good it feels to have this wonderful energetic balance that the Fifth Ray provides.

(Wait one minute.)

Take a gentle breath in and, as you do, begin to allow your consciousness to return to your physical body. Take another gentle breath in and gently wiggle your fingers and your toes, feeling your consciousness more fully returning. Take one more gentle breath in and feel your arms and your legs. When you are ready, gently open your eyes and return to this place and this time feeling relaxed, refreshed, and better than you have felt all day.

Welcome back! Keep in mind that you don't have to focus for a long time on the chakras that you feel are already balanced. If you feel the balance in any one, you can pretty much skip over it and move on to the next one.

CHAPTER 5

The Sixth Ray
Devotion and Idealism

"All these energies that we have spoken about flow through you. Becoming aware of them is simply a way to raise that consciousness to enlighten you to the power that you work with, that you avail yourself of. In every moment, you choose the energies that you bring to your being, and by so doing, you affect the energies of everything in your reality."

– The Team

The Sixth Ray, the Ray of Devotion and Idealism, can be found in varying degrees in practically everyone on the planet. The problem is that it can be easily overdone, and the results are less than positive. Here is how the Team first described this Ray.

> *The Sixth Ray is the Ray of Devotion and Idealism, and you can visualize it as indigo blue energy. The Sixth Ray has a very precise focus in its energy, and people that carry a lot of this energy tend to be obsessive. It has addictive qualities in regards to religion; it can create an energy of zealous belief. It can be used to put things on automatic.*

I'm sure you can look back at history and find examples of religious extremism. Think about the Crusades or the Inquisition of the Middle Ages. Look around the globe today, and you will find examples of religious extremism. The good news is that this energy can be refined and have a very positive effect on us. Here is the Team's explanation.

> *You can bring this Ray in, focus on it, and envision it growing lighter. For this energy is a very heavy energy in your earthly environment, and it tends to cling. Yet by raising it up in a lighter, less addictive vibration, it can help focus your intentions and your objectives.*

This is exactly how we will use this energy. Before we can achieve our goals and objectives, we must first define them and clarify them. As we complete the guided journey for the Sixth Ray, think about the goals and the objectives you have set for yourself and whether you have a clear idea of what they are. But before we take that guided journey, let's do this next exercise where we will simply connect with the energy of the Sixth Ray.

Listen, Feel, and Connect Exercise 3:
THE SIXTH RAY

This exercise is similar to the two preceding exercises. We will once again use a painting by Melinda Radcliffe to help us connect with the energy of the Sixth Ray, with music composed and performed by Richard Shulman to accompany the visual connection. If you have the painting and the music available to you, that is great. Alternatively, you can go to my YouTube channel and watch and listen to a video I have prepared that has the music and the painting combined. Visit thetwelverays.com to find the link.

If you've had the opportunity to complete the previous two exercises, then you should be familiar with the procedure. Remember that the goal here is simply to connect with the energy of the Sixth Ray. All you need to do is stay focused in the present moment. Don't think about what you did yesterday. Don't think about what you are going to do later today. Think about right here and right now. As you begin the exercise, allow yourself to focus on whatever strikes you most powerfully, the music or the painting. Then allow your consciousness to gradually become aware of the other part of the exercise. So if you find the music more interesting at first, go with that and gradually allow yourself to become more aware of the painting.

Again, I suggest that you have writing implements at your disposal. You will want to record any insights that you receive as soon as you finish the exercise. This exercise is about ten minutes long. When you can sit uninterrupted for about ten minutes, find yourself a comfortable place to sit and begin the exercise. And remember to have fun!

Start the music and allow yourself to focus for ten minutes.

Welcome back. The goal of this exercise is to simply become familiar with the energy of the Sixth Ray. We didn't have any defined goals other than that for this exercise. Two guided journeys in this chapter will be more focused on practical outcomes. Before we begin our guided journeys, let's delve into the concepts of devotion and idealism a little more deeply.

Devotion

Devotion is perhaps one of the most defining of all the human characteristics. When I think of devotion, the first thought that comes to my mind is parental devotion, specifically maternal devotion. How many times have you heard a mother say that she is willing to give her life for her children? But devotion to our children is way more than that, as any parent understands. Becoming a parent changes you for the rest of your life. All parents are charged with the welfare of their children. We look out for them and nurture them and protect them with the intention that their lives will, in some way, shape, or form, be more wondrous than our own lives.

Parenthood is not possible for everyone. Other forms of devotion are certainly all around us. People become devoted to causes that become the focus of their lives: the environment, world hunger, clean water, animal rights, the list goes on and on. So many of us are involved in causes, and it is making a difference.

The problem is that devotion can sometimes lead to becoming unbalanced. Discerning whether you are unbalanced with a certain cause or activity is, of course, a very personal assessment. In our next guided journey, we will focus on where we might be unbalanced in respect to the amount of attention we give to a cause or our roles. But before we do that, let's spend just a little bit of time on idealism.

Idealism

When I think of idealism, I think of taking something that already exists and improving it for the benefit of all concerned. It usually involves some big picture concepts like freedom, equality, democracy, education, health care, or the environment. How often have you heard someone say, "Well, in an ideal world, such and such might be the case." The inference being that it is not the case because we don't live in an ideal world.

Many individuals are pursuing their personal ambitions that are based in idealism. I can think of dozens of professions that are based on idealism. Can you? One of the first that comes to mind is teaching. I'm quite sure that most teachers believe that knowledge is a very desirable goal to pursue. So they work to help us discover knowledge. How about everyone working to protect us? All the firefighters, police, first responders, and military? Aren't they pursuing the ideals of freedom, safety, and democracy? I think they are. I would also include scientists of all disciplines. They are in pursuit of the truth for the betterment of all.

There are more than those that I have mentioned. I'm sure you will agree that this is a pretty big list. Anyone in these professions can possibly become unbalanced, as shown in television dramas. This is where the Sixth Ray can be helpful. Regardless of how much of the Sixth Ray you may be accessing now, you can fine-tune it to be lighter and more balanced. And that is what our next guided journey will help us to achieve.

 Guided Journey 3: THE SIXTH RAY

Our discussion about the Sixth Ray has focused on two seemingly separate issues—clarifying our goals and objectives and becoming energetically rebalanced. And while these two considerations may seem unrelated, they are really very similar. You might think of them as two sides of the same coin. If you don't have a clear understanding of your goals and objectives, how do you know if you are spending the right amount of your personal energy on them? Likewise, if you are spending too much of your energy on them, are your goals and objectives clear and reasonable?

This is where discernment kicks in. Only you can decide if your goals and objectives are where they need to be. Only you can decide if you are spending the right amount of your personal energy on them. A question that might come to mind is, "How do I know?" That is what this next exercise is all about. Take the time to work through it, and you will have a much better understanding of where you stand in relation to your goals and objectives.

If you are not really clear about your personal goals or where to focus your energy, then perhaps you should skip to Alternate Guided Journey 3 on page 50. Then when you have gained a certain level of clarity about your personal goals, you can come back to this mediation to help you fine-tune your involvement.

Hopefully by now, you are comfortable with the format of the guided journeys. Before we begin this one, I'd like to go over something that the Team mentioned about this Sixth Ray, that this Ray is "a very heavy energy in your earthly environment." They suggest that we need to raise it up and make it lighter. So during this next journey, one of the goals is to raise up our individual Sixth Ray energy.

We do that through our intentions. The choices we make are all based on our motivations. The highest level of motivation is love. The lowest level of motivation is fear. While fear is a good motivator in times when we feel in danger, love is a much better motivator. Unfortunately, it seems that the messages of fear are all too frequently used in today's marketing messages.

The way to lighten the energy of this Ray is to transmute the fears associated with our motivations to something more closely aligned to love. We will do this by opening our hearts to the energy of the Ray we are working with. We all know the difference between being motivated by love and being motivated by anything else. Creating from that place of love, the heart, takes us back to the Second Ray, the Ray of Love and Wisdom. Creating with love is part of our Spiritual Heritage.

Like the preceding ones, this journey is rather long, so I suggest you read it through first, then record yourself reading it. If you prefer, a recording is available on my website, thetwelverays.com. You will need about ten minutes of uninterrupted time. Make sure you have something to write with and on. When you are ready, find yourself a comfortable place to relax and be seated. If some other position is more comfortable for you, then by all means do what feels best. Let's begin.

Take a gentle, relaxing breath. Breathe in relaxing, fresh air and breathe out any tension or stress you may be feeling. Take another gentle breath in, relaxing, and gently letting go. Good. Now take one more gentle breath in and exhale any remaining stress or tension you may be feeling. Very good.

You are about to call on the energy of the Sixth Ray, the Ray of Devotion and Idealism. Many individuals use this energy in creative fashions each and every day. Just take a moment and consider what you are passionate about and, as you do, begin to feel yourself surrounded by this beautiful indigo blue energy of the Sixth Ray. Feel it move through you and allow it to move into your heart center.

If you are fortunate enough to be able to engage with the thing that you are passionate about every day, then focus on this energy and make it lighter by blending it with love. Think of those things that you love: your significant other, your children, your family, your household pets, your favorite hobbies. Allow those feelings of love to be blended into this energy of the Sixth Ray. Perhaps you are thinking of a special musical piece, a song or a symphony, or a special place like the mountains or the ocean. Allow that love to fill your heart and blend it into the energy of the Sixth Ray. And as you do, you will feel it becoming lighter and lighter. Very good.

By blending these energies, it becomes easier for you to balance your passions, along with all the other energies that you use on a daily basis. This balance is so important, for you never want to be so involved with one thing, that other aspects of your life suffer. Too many of us let our passions for our jobs take away from spending time with our loved ones. Too many of us sacrifice one thing for the other. By blending our passion with our heartfelt love, we help to create a balance that allows us to spend the right amount of time and energy on those things that are most important to us.

Feel this energy of the Sixth Ray continue to blend with your heart center, with the love that you hold in your heart. Feel how calm and peaceful you feel knowing that you have balanced this energy of devotion and idealism with your love.

As you find yourself in this peaceful place, consider what your goals and objectives are for whatever it is that you are passionate about. Do you have clarity around them? If not, this is a perfect opportunity to focus on those goals and use your imagination to allow yourself the freedom to envision clearly what those goals could be. Don't worry about being practical. That will come later. Use this opportunity to consider what would make you happy.

(Wait one minute.)

Use that feeling of happiness and send it out to the universe, along with your clear vision of your goals. Be prepared to take action as the universe responds to you. This is how we all create our personal realities. We create our goals and our personal objectives through our thoughts, and we send them out into the universe, and the universe responds back to us. Our role is to recognize the universe's responses and take action to make our thoughts, our goals, and our objectives our reality.

In a moment, we will begin our journey back to a fully awake state of consciousness. Before we do, focus and remember how wonderful it feels to be in such a calm and peaceful place. When you balance the energy of the Sixth Ray with your heartfelt love, you raise it up to be lighter and more balanced. You will find it easier to be happy and successful as you pursue your passions.

Now, take a gentle breath in and, as you do, begin to allow your consciousness to return to your physical body. Take another gentle breath in and gently begin to move your fingers and your toes. As you take another gentle breath in, allow your consciousness to return more fully to your physical body, feeling your arms and your legs. And when you are ready, gently open your eyes and return to this place and this time feeling refreshed, relaxed, and better than you have felt all day.

Welcome back. Take this time to write down any insights that you received during this guided journey. Feel free to do this guided journey as often as you would like. It may take more than one experience to receive the information that you are seeking.

 ## Alternate Guided Journey 3: THE SIXTH RAY

This alternative guided journey is very similar to the one above. The difference is this journey is intended for individuals who are not yet as fully involved in their passions as they would like to be—anyone working in a job that is not really their passion or who has other obligations that prevent them from following their passion. Use the Sixth Ray to gain clarity on your goals. Create an image of the perfect situation that would allow you to pursue your passion. Don't worry about the practical aspects. You will use the Third Ray to help you develop your plan for manifesting that perfect scenario.

Before we begin this one, remember what the Team mentioned about this Sixth Ray: it is "a very heavy energy in your Earthly environment." They suggest that we need to raise it up and make it lighter. So during this next journey, one of the goals is to raise up our individual Sixth Ray energy.

We do that through our intentions. The choices we make are all based on our motivations. The highest level of motivation is love. The lowest level of motivation is fear. While fear is a good motivator in times when we feel in danger, love is a much better motivator. Unfortunately, it seems that the messages of fear are all too frequently used in today's marketing messages.

The way to lighten the energy of this Ray is to transmute fears associated with our motivations to something more closely aligned to love. We will do this by opening our hearts to the energy of the Ray we are working with. We all know the difference between being motivated by love and being motivated by anything else. Creating from that place of love, the heart, takes us back to the Second Ray, the Ray of Love and Wisdom. Creating with love is part of our Spiritual Heritage.

Like the preceding ones, this journey is rather long, so I suggest you read it through first, then record yourself reading it. If you prefer, a recording is available on my website, thetwelverays.com. You will need about ten minutes of uninterrupted time. Make sure you have something to write with and on. When you are ready, find yourself a comfortable place to relax and be seated. If some other position is more comfortable for you, then by all means do what feels best. Let's begin.

Take a gentle, relaxing breath. Breathe in relaxing, fresh air and breathe out any tension or stress you may be feeling. Take another gentle breath in, relaxing, and gently letting go. Good. Now take one more gentle breath in and exhale any remaining stress or tension you may be feeling. Very good.

You are about to call on the energy of the Sixth Ray, the Ray of Devotion and Idealism. Many individuals use this energy in creative fashions each and every day. Just take a moment and think about what you are passionate about and, as you do, begin to feel yourself surrounded by this beautiful indigo blue energy of the Sixth Ray. Feel it move through you and allow it to move into your heart center.

Allow yourself to imagine what being involved with your passion would look like. What would it look like on a daily basis? And as you imagine yourself doing that, working with your passion on a regular basis, allow that image to become one of your goals. Allow it to become a clear objective for you. Don't worry about the practical aspects right now. Just stay focused on the goal. How does it feel to imagine yourself involved with your passion? Use that feeling to help you make this goal of yours a reality. Send this feeling of working with your passion out into the universe and be prepared to take action as the universe responds to you.

This is how we all create our personal realities. We create our goals and our personal objectives through our thoughts, and we send them out into the universe, and the universe responds back to us. Our role is to recognize the responses from the universe and take action to make our thoughts, goals, and objectives into our reality.

Now as you hold that image of you working with the things you are passionate about, ask yourself if there is any resistance to manifesting this goal. Ask yourself if you feel any resistance to any changes that might be required in order for you to realize this goal. You may have a limiting belief that is keeping you from your new goal. Perhaps you think that you cannot make enough money doing what it is that you are passionate about. You might think that you do not know how to go about finding out if there are really jobs like the one that would allow you to work with your passion. Maybe you believe that change is hard. Let's see if there may be resistance to change.

Remember back to when you worked with the energy of the First Ray to help you identify the source of your resistance to change. Call upon that energy now, the beautiful red energy of the First Ray, the Ray of Divine Will, and let it descend around you in a column of light. And when you feel yourself surrounded by the energy of the First Ray, ask if there is indeed resistance to achieving your new goal. All you want to do here is identify the source of any possible resistance. If nothing comes to you, then good. But if you sense there is something causing resistance on your part, ask for clarity in seeing exactly what it is.

And if you have detected any resistance to change, remember that all we want to do right now is identify the source. We will subsequently use the Third Ray to develop a plan to move beyond it.

(Wait one minute.)

In a moment, we will begin our journey back to a fully awakened state of consciousness. Take this moment and remember how wonderful it feels to be able to picture yourself being more involved with your passion. And if you have uncovered any resistance to your new goal, by using the Third Ray, the Ray of Active Intelligence, you will be able to create a plan to move beyond it. It is now time to begin your journey back to full waking consciousness.

Take a gentle breath in and, as you do, begin to allow your consciousness to return to your physical body. Take another gentle breath in and gently begin to move your fingers and your toes. As you take another gentle breath in, allow your consciousness to return more fully to your physical body, feeling your arms and your legs. And when you are ready, gently open your eyes and return to this place and this time feeling refreshed, relaxed, and better than you have felt all day.

Welcome back. Take this time to write down any insights that you received during this guided journey. Take special note of anything that you identified as a source of resistance to change. You will want to work with that using the Third Ray.

"Step outside ritual, open to feel and hear what others have failed to grasp …. It is a time for you to transition in love, and as with any growth, there will be challenges to move away from old beliefs and rituals. This is a time for you to put away the old and to embrace the challenges and opportunities of a new awareness."

– The Team

CHAPTER 6

Ritual and Ceremony

Before we consider the next Ray, I would like to have a brief discussion about the name of this Ray. When you look back at the earliest texts that talk about the Seven Rays, the Seventh Ray is almost always described as the Ray of Ceremonial Order or Magic. I like to use the word "ritual" instead of ceremonial order. Here is how Wikipedia defines ritual:

> *A ritual is a sequence of activities involving gestures, words, and objects, performed in a sequestered place, and performed according to set sequence. Rituals may be prescribed by the traditions of a community, including a religious community. Rituals are characterized but not defined by formalism, traditionalism, invariance, rule-governance, sacral symbolism, and performance.*
>
> *Rituals are a feature of all known human societies. They include not only the worship rites and sacraments of organized religions and cults, but also rites of passage, atonement and purification rites, oaths of allegiance, dedication ceremonies, coronations and presidential inaugurations, marriages, funerals, and more. Even common actions like hand shaking and saying "hello" may be termed rituals.*

Something about rituals makes them very appealing. And without going into a discussion of neuroplasticity and psychology, certain rituals seem to be very beneficial, while others are not. I'll let you be the judge of what you find helpful and what you don't. Many rituals, such as hand shaking or saying hello, become habituated patterns, and we do them without even thinking about them. Likewise, the response to such rituals can be given without much thought or even truthfulness. How often have you responded to, "How are you?" with an automatic response regardless of how you really feel?

Think about your morning routine on a workday as a ritual. More than likely, you get out of bed and do the same thing day in and day out without having to think much about it. That is probably a good thing, because it leaves you free to think about other things like what you have planned during the day. Your daily commute is probably another ritual. You likely get to where you need to be the same way every day. Again, you don't have to put much thought into it.

Rituals are a part of our everyday life. Generally speaking, they can be trusted to lead to a predictable outcome. Rituals are used to preserve the status quo and rarely bring forth innovation. Some people believe that rituals can actually inhibit innovation.

Prayer is used by some religions as a primary ritual for worship. In the religious tradition in which I was raised, repetition of the same memorized prayers was stressed. This repetition of the same prayer over and over again is perhaps best embodied in the rosary. My personal experience with this method was that repetition led me to no longer really pay attention to the intention of the prayer. Also, I never really learned to pray from my heart or to use my own words in prayer. When you learn to pray from your heart using your own words, are you still following the rituals?

If we do not wish to continue to be restrained by outmoded rituals, what do we use in their place? We embrace new processes. I would suggest that when you use your own words in prayer, you are following a process instead of a ritual.

Processes allow you to vary the elements that are added to yield different results. Think of your kitchen blender as a process of liquefaction. You can put almost anything into it, and the process chops it up and turns it to liquid. Fill it with ice, add some strawberry jam and some milk, turn it on, and you have a strawberry milkshake. Think of the Seventh Ray as a process to integrate past experiences into the totality of your life experiences. We add some stored emotions, combine them with the Seventh Ray, and we get something new, something that becomes integrated into who you are.

When you read the guided exercises included here, please do not think of them as formal rituals that should be followed to the letter. They are meant to be introductory approaches to using the Rays. Please feel free to make changes and adjustments to them any way you see fit. This is all about you exercising your innate abilities as the creator of your own reality. You will never be comfortable with your creative abilities if you continue to follow what someone else has given you. I am providing guidelines to help you start. As you gain familiarity with the Rays, I hope you will become more and more creative with them.

So if we no longer refer to the Seventh Ray by its old name, what do we call it now? The Team refers to the Seventh Ray as the Gateway into Awareness, or alternatively as the Violet Flame. The term "Violet Flame" has been used for several decades to refer to the Seventh Ray. I have divided the information about the Seventh Ray into two sections. The first section presents the Seventh Ray as the more traditional understanding of it as the Violet Flame. Although the way it was presented through Guy Ballard and Mark and Elizabeth Clare Prophet was very ritualized, it can also be used as a process. And that is what I have presented first.

When the new Rays (Rays Eight through Ray Twelve) were made available to humanity, the role of the Seventh Ray was further clarified as being the Gateway into Awareness. When we use the Seventh Ray as the Gateway into Awareness, it helps us to open to the "grander, greater expression of what you know yourself to be." It helps us to break through the limiting beliefs we have about ourselves. As we embrace this grander vision of ourselves, we raise up our personal energetic fields, and this opens us to new insights about ourselves and the universe we live in.

An alternative guided journey is offered in chapter 8. The expansion of our own beliefs about who we are and what we are capable of creating in this dimension may be new to some. It was certainly new for me. When we step into something that is new, we often have a certain degree of uncertainty that goes along with it. I think that is quite normal and to be expected.

My suggestion is to proceed at your own comfortable pace. When we open ourselves to personal expansion, we often have a lot of moving parts that require adjustments and alignments. We have our personal beliefs about ourselves, our comfort level in giving and receiving love, our beliefs about healing ourselves, and many more. All the while, we need to maintain our relationships with those around us. There is no need to rush any of this. No one needs that added pressure. We will talk more about this in chapter 8.

Let's begin working with the Seventh Ray in the context of the traditional sense of the Violet Flame.

CHAPTER 7

The Seventh Ray
The Violet Flame of Saint Germain

"The Violet Flame—call on the Violet Flame when you are ready, when those you work with are ready to acknowledge the resistance that they hold, when they are ready to accept what they are. You may find that it is hard to believe that most people, [we] would dare say most people on your planet, have yet to agree, to acknowledge their own perfection, their potential. They do not understand they do not have to suffer. They do not understand they do not have to live in difficulty. Jesus never desired to suffer, never desired for His people, all of mankind, to acknowledge any suffering from Him. When you release this illusion, you open a door to releasing all discomfort, all pain. You open a new door to draw in more love, more light. We have an opportunity here in this life, not the next—in this life, in this experience—to be in unconditional love, to understand the joy, the simplicity, the harmony."

– The Team

When Julie and I first received the information on the Seventh Ray, I had heard about Saint Germain, but never really took the time to delve into his story too deeply. In a broader sense, Saint Germain is commonly associated with the healing arts, kind of a patron saint of the healing arts (no pun intended). Numerous stories exist about Saint Germain living for a long time in eighteenth and nineteenth century Europe and being friends with influential members of society, including kings and queens. He is reported to have been a Master of Alchemy.

In more modern times, Mount Shasta in northern California is said to be a focal point for Saint Germain and the energy of the Violet Flame. Guy Ballard claims to have met Saint Germain while hiking on Mount Shasta in the 1930s. In his book *Unveiled Mysteries*, Ballard describes his many encounters with Saint Germain. He authored several more books about the Violet Flame and went on to form the "I AM" movement. Mark and Elizabeth Clare Prophet wrote about the Violet Flame extensively in the mid-to-later parts of the twentieth century.

My feeling is that those were messages for that time. The energies have shifted substantially, and what was relevant then is not necessarily relevant today. What I mean is the manner in which individuals have worked with the Seventh Ray in the past was appropriate for that time period. Some may choose to continue to work with the Violet Flame in the same ritualized manner. And that is fine. What I am presenting here is a way to work with the Seventh Rays without all the ritual associated with it.

I had the opportunity to attend a workshop at Mt. Shasta back in 2005. The workshop was presented by Jessie Ayani, a gifted teacher and author. I highly recommend both her workshops and her books. I could feel the energy of the Violet Flame while I was out there even before I had connected it to the Seventh Ray.

The Seventh Ray, the Gateway into Awareness, is different from the preceding three Rays of Attributes. Everyone has some of each of those three Rays in them, and we use those energies to create our everyday experiences. As I indicated in the previous chapter, we use the Seventh Ray as more of a process, and we use it in two different ways. The first approach is to use the Seventh Ray to integrate our past experiences. Human beings tend to store emotions in the physical body, especially unresolved emotional experiences that still leave us uncomfortable, those we haven't yet integrated into our personalities.

Pleasant experiences that we find very joyful are generally integrated easily. These experiences are resolved. The ones that I am focusing on are the ones that still evoke unpleasant emotions when you think about them. And I'm not talking about all unpleasant experiences. I'm only including those experiences that are still "active." The ones that are difficult to move beyond even though they may be stored away deeply and not often thought of. They can still be considered active. They are the ones that have not yet been integrated.

These experiences are generally stored in the body along with the emotions that accompanied them. They are usually disruptive to the normal functioning of wherever they are stored and can become symptomatic if they are not dealt with. An entire subsection of craniosacral therapy is devoted to working with these unresolved experiences. It is called SomatoEmotional Release. The unresolved emotions stored in the body are referred to as "energy cysts." I prefer employing the Seventh Ray when working with unresolved, stored emotions.

Before we learn how to use this Ray to process our unresolved emotions, let's do a quick exercise to connect with the energy of this Ray.

 Listen, Feel, and Connect Exercise 4:
THE SEVENTH RAY

This exercise takes about ten minutes and involves the artwork and the music associated with the Seventh Ray. We are not going to actually work with any unresolved emotions in this exercise. All we want to do here is listen, feel, and connect with the Seventh Ray. Just notice if you are attracted to the music first or the artwork first. Allow yourself to connect with the energy of the Ray and go deeper into it. Be aware of the insights you are getting. Have a pen and paper ready to capture your insights at the end of this exercise.

The Seventh Ray is called the Violet Flame and is associated with the Ascended Master Saint Germain. To prepare yourself for this exercise, have a copy of the painting in front of you along with the music. Alternatively, I created a video that has the painting and the music together. Go to my YouTube channel and click on the Seventh Ray. Visit my website, thetwelverays.com, to find the link.

Start the music and allow yourself to focus for ten minutes.

Welcome back. I included these exercises in the book because I believe they are very helpful in the process of connecting to the Rays. I can only suggest that you take advantage of them. Feel free to do them as often as you like. I always find something new and different each time I listen and go deeper into the artwork and the music.

I previously mentioned there are two ways to work with the Seventh Ray. The more traditional approach, working with the Violet Flame, is what we will be doing in the next guided journey. Before we do that, let me share with you a little more about the Seventh Ray.

The Violet Flame

Quoting once again from my book, *The Reality of Your Greatness; A Personal Journey through the Twelve Rays*, this is how the Team first introduced the Seventh Ray:

The Seventh Ray is a violet, a violet energy that we call the Gateway into Awareness. It is the energy that is used to dissolve the weightiness of past experience and transmute that energy up into a higher vibration so that you might advance in your evolution of Spirit. You may picture this in meditation as a Violet Flame, and move it down through the denser energies, through your chakras, raising them up, opening them to the grander, greater expression of what you know yourself to be.

In this chapter, we are working with the aspect of the Seventh Ray that involves dissolving the weightiness of past experiences and integrating those experiences into our personalities. These past experiences are the emotional energy cysts that are stored in the body. But since energy is never lost, when the energy cysts dissolve, they are really transmuting to a higher vibration, a higher emotional state that is free of judgment and lower-level emotions such as pain, suffering, guilt, and anger.

As you integrate these higher vibrations, you advance in your evolution by opening up to a grander, greater expression of who you really are and what you are really able to become. You use the Seventh Ray in a two-step process that allows you to process the weightiness of past experience and integrate each past experience into your total experience. As you process each one, you raise your individual energetic levels up, which opens you to evolving your Spirit. That is what makes the Seventh Ray unique among all the Rays.

Guided Journey 4: THE SEVENTH RAY

In this guided journey, we will use the Seventh Ray to work with the active energy cysts in the physical body. You don't need any special training in order to be successful with this technique. All you need is (1) the desire to release yourself from these lower-level energies that are trapped in the body and (2) the belief that you are in control of your own reality. Part of that belief is that you can heal yourself by rebalancing your personal energy.

At the end of the guided journey, you are asked to bring in the Eighth Ray. The Eighth Ray is the Cleansing Ray, and I purposely haven't mentioned it because it bridges both the Rays of Attributes and the Rays of Soul Integration. We will work with it solely in its role as the Cleansing Ray here. It has a violet and green color and is used with the Seventh Ray to cleanse, refresh, and rebalance the energy in our physical bodies and more. For now, I don't think we need to get into it any more than that.

This guided journey is not as complex as the previous ones. It may take the same amount of time, but it is very straightforward. It starts out like the previous journeys, with relaxation breathing. I will then help you to connect with the consciousness of your body, which is really the basis to most all body work. In most cases, the body has been waiting to make this connection. When you connect to the consciousness of the body with your intention to help it to heal, you enter into a healing partnership with your body.

Once you feel this connection, we will move on to scanning your body to identify areas where you feel emotions are ready to be worked with. Let the consciousness of your body guide you. This is a good time to get out of your head and into your heart. You are not here to direct. You are here to help.

It might still be a good idea to read the entire journey over first and then record it so that you can follow along when you play it back. Or visit my website, thetwelverays.com, and listen to my recording of it. You may not be familiar with some of these techniques at first. Do whatever allows you to feel relaxed and confident. Make sure you have about ten minutes of uninterrupted time for yourself and, of course, a pen and paper nearby to capture any insights you may receive. Here we go.

Let's begin by taking a deep, gentle breath in, and with each breath in feel relaxing, fresh air, and with each breath out exhale any stress or tension that you may be feeling. Now take another gentle breath in feeling that relaxing fresh air and exhaling out any stress or tension. Now take one more gentle breath in going deeper and deeper into relaxation and breathing out any remaining stress or tension. Good.

Take a moment and set your intention for healing. Come into this guided journey with the intention to help your body heal. You are in contact with the energy of the Seventh Ray. Your body consciousness is in contact with the stored emotions that you will work with. Working as a team, you will bring these two together and be able to facilitate the healing that is necessary.

Think about the complexity of your physical body. Think about all the processes that are involved in keeping you healthy and happy. A consciousness within you has the responsibility for your well-being. Let's call this your body consciousness. We're going to take a moment to connect with this body consciousness. The way that we're going to do that is simply through our focused attention.

So quietly in your mind, say to yourself, "I wish to connect with my body consciousness." Always remember to listen whenever you make such a statement for yourself. Remember to listen and react. State once again your intention—to connect to your body consciousness for the purpose of working with your emotions that are trapped within your physical body. And, again, quietly say to your body consciousness, "I want to help release. I want to help process these emotions that are ready to be transmuted to a higher level. I want to help integrate these past experiences."

When you are ready, ask your body consciousness, "Are you ready to proceed?" Listen for an answer. Hopefully, you will receive a response right away. If you don't hear a response, simply repeat the question again. If you still don't hear a response, ask if there's something your body consciousness needs before continuing and, again, listen for the answer. If there is no response to that question, then decide whether to continue or to try again later. After all, this is a new technique, and sometimes it takes a while for your body consciousness to understand your intention.

Assuming that your body consciousness has agreed to continue, envision a column of violet energy above your head and allow it to slowly move down into your head. Allow it to move down your neck into your abdomen. Continue to allow it to move to your hips, your legs, and all the way down to your feet. Now send it down into Mother Earth. Very good.

Bring your awareness back to the top of your head and slowly allow your awareness to descend from the top of your head down through your head, into your neck and throat, down into your shoulders. Any place that you find something of interest (and that is for you to define what something of interest means) stop and take note. You may want to continue on and scan your entire body, or stop here and work with this energy here. Either way is fine.

If you continue on, allow your awareness to move through your entire body. Allow it to move down into your abdomen, down into your hips, down to your legs, and into your feet. Remember to include your arms and your hands. Now, decide which area you think would be the best place to begin. It may be either the first place that you stopped, or the place that you sense is ready to release.

Bring your awareness to the part of your body where you sense that there is energy willing to be transmuted. Direct the Violet Flame to transmute it to a higher vibration and integrate it into your personality. Continue directing the Violet Flame to that area and wait until you feel the process is complete. If this is your first time working with this process, then I suggest you stop here and move on to the next step. If, however, you would like to continue on, rescan your body, starting at the top of your head and repeat the process.

The next step is to bring in the Eighth Ray, the Cleansing Ray, and envision it as a column of violet and green energy descending from above your head. Let it gently wash all the way through your body. This energy will work with more than just your physical body. Allow the energy of the Eighth Ray to wash thorough you, cleansing and refreshing your energy as it does. Allow it to flush all the way down into Mother Earth. Good.

In a moment we will begin to return to your full waking consciousness. But before that, know that you can bring back your entire memory of what you have experienced with this session of the Seventh Ray. You can remember all that you experienced, even the insights you gained along the way. You return with this past experience integrated into your total life experience.

Take a gentle breath in and, as you do, begin to allow your consciousness to return to your physical body. Take another gentle breath in and gently begin to move your fingers and your toes. As you take another gentle breath in, allow your consciousness to return more fully to your physical body, feeling your arms and your legs. When you are ready, gently open your eyes and return to this place and this time feeling refreshed, relaxed, and better than you have felt all day.

Welcome back. Take this time to write down any insights that you received during this guided journey. Take special note of anything that you identified as ready to be transmuted but weren't able to complete. You will want to keep that in mind when you do this journey again.

Repeat Often

This guided journey is meant to be repeated often. Once you get familiar with the basic concept, you will see that it is pretty straightforward. You simply relax, connect with your body consciousness, ask it to help identify emotions that are ready to be transmuted and integrated, and bring in the Seventh Ray to provide the shift. Then bring in the Eighth Ray to cleanse, refresh, and rebalance.

Each time you complete this guided journey, it will have an impact on the remaining emotions that are trapped in the body. It is kind of like an onion.

Once you peel back the outer layer, you expose inner layers that are now ready to be worked with. You are in charge of the timing. Find your own pace and don't try to rush it. This isn't a race.

Let's move on to part two of the Seventh Ray.

"Allow your heart to be lifted. Allow yourself to feel connected. Allow yourself to feel a part of something that can never end, that can never be taken from you, that you can't destroy."

– The Team

CHAPTER 8

Separation and Connection

When you look at yourself in the mirror, what do you see? You see an image reflected of your physical self. Many individuals believe they are just a physical being. Using your eyes alone, you are not apt to see anything more in your reflection.

In reality, we all have two aspects to our physical being. We are both of this physical dimension and of a different nonphysical dimension. Let's refer to this nonphysical dimension as a spiritual dimension. So when you see yourself reflected in the mirror, understand that there are really two of you in your body—your physical self and spiritual self joined together. I refer to the spiritual self as the soul-level consciousness. Without getting too bogged down in metaphysical jargon, I define the soul-level conscious as that level of consciousness that is you outside of this human experience. You existed before you incarnated as a human and you will return to that existence after this human experience.

Our physical bodies are divinely designed to house our spiritual or energetic selves, our soul-level consciousness, in this dimension. Many of us have little appreciation for the complexities of the physical body. I don't want to delve too deeply into the magnificence of the physical body here, but the average body contains 37 trillion cells, and each cell contains consciousness. It is easy to think of our bodies as relatively crowded places. As a matter of fact, I think of the human body as a universe all its own.

We are mostly unaware of the millions and millions of processes that are operating within our bodies practically nonstop—respiration, circulation, and cell reproduction, to name just a few. A critical thing to keep in mind is that we create the environments in which the universes inside us exists. We do this through the care that we give our bodies and, most importantly, though our mental states. Our thoughts influence our emotions, which release hormones into our bodies that trigger automatic responses. When we feel love, our cells feel loved. When we feel stress and fear, our cells are stressed and fearful. We have control over our internal environment.

You can think of these stored emotions that we have been working with as internal pollution. Working with the Seventh Ray helps to clean up that pollution.

Separation

As you've read in previous chapters, the world we live in is a world of duality, a world of opposites—light and dark, male and female, hot and cold, and on and on. Separation represents a duality with connection. One of the most striking aspects of this physical dimension is the potential to feel like a stand-alone individual disconnected from almost everything. Combine this with human emotions, another unique characteristic of this physical dimension, and you create the opportunity to feel loneliness.

Our first experience of physical separation is at birth. After spending nine months attached to another living organism, birth sets us on a path of individuation. As we learn about the world outside of the protection of our mother's bodies, systems are activated to support our independent functioning. We breathe for ourselves. We begin to process sensory input, especially from our eyes. We express ourselves through sound.

The older we get, the more we experience the fullness of the human environment. One of the wonderful benefits that we experience in this dimension is free will. We are able to make our own choices and experience the results of our choices. We learn through experience that we truly do create our own realities.

As we mature, the number of personal relationships that we have increases. This is another one of those special opportunities for experience that this physical dimension affords us. Human relationships are among the most complex phenomena that we encounter on Earth. We experience love through our relationships, but we also experience loss through them. And sooner or later, this leads to a sense of loneliness. Loneliness is an emotion that almost all of us humans feel at one time or another. And planet Earth, because of its dense, physical energy, is about the best place to come to and have these experiences of loneliness.

Connection

As I mentioned earlier, connection is the opposite of separation. It seems that many of our human relationships start with auspicious beginnings, but regretfully end up falling apart. I think it is fair to say that most people have more relationships that have faded away than have endured. The ones that are maintained generally have some special characteristics to them like family, childhood friends, schoolmates, and colleagues. These relationships are sources of great joy for us, and we consider them to be precious.

Earlier, I made reference to the physical separation that takes place at birth. Another type of separation happens at birth that almost all of us are unaware of. In reality, it is not so much a separation as it is a reduction in consciousness based upon the physical characteristics of this dimension. It is often said that when we are born, we pass through a cloud of forgetfulness. This is often misinterpreted as a separation from soul-level consciousness. This is, however, just an illusion of separation.

We do indeed experience a reduction in consciousness, and this is referred to as spiritual discord. In essence, spiritual discord is the feeling of not having the same abilities here on Earth as we have in other dimensions. And this is very real. The good news is that most often spiritual discord is not consciously remembered during a lifetime. It can potentially become an issue as individuals begin to open to a greater understanding of who they really are, which leads us to the topic of spiritual connection.

As we open to our personal realities beyond this dimension, we remember our connections to soul-level consciousness. We look for ways to strengthen that memory of connection. That is exactly what we can use the Seventh Ray for. We use the Seventh Ray to strengthen our awareness of our true selves. The next chapter contains a guided journey that is specifically designed to help connect and strengthen your connection to your soul-level consciousness. This is the New Awareness that the higher Rays give us access to.

Consider for a moment what this means. We can actually experience ourselves as always having been connected to soul-level consciousness, while living in a dimension that has been designed to create an illusion of physical and spiritual separation. When we embrace our Spiritual Heritage, we have the opportunity to experience connection in a world that has by and large only known separation.

I believe this is the next step forward for humankind. Consider the possibilities that this opens up!

"It is hard to believe in something new until you are willing to let go of something old."

– The Team

CHAPTER 9

The Seventh Ray Gateway into Awareness

Imagine that spring is about to burst forth, and it is the first spring you have ever experienced. I could tell you that all those trees that look dead are actually alive and are about to put forth blooms in a dazzling array of colors and shapes. And as the blossoms are maturing, they all sprout leaves that bring new growth to all the plants.

Likewise, I could point out the brown grass that surrounds so many homes and tell you that the grass is about to turn the most vibrant green you have ever seen, and it will grow and grow and grow. If you do not cut it, it will grow as high as three feet tall.

And then there are all the flowers in the ground. Last year's beautiful spring bulbs are nowhere to be seen. But soon the green leaves will spring up, and the flowers will follow. They are augmented by the beautiful flowers on the bushes and the trees. These perennials are reinforced with annuals as soon as the threat of frost is over.

If you had never experienced a spring before, would you believe me? You may or you may not believe me, but once you have experienced your first spring, it is very hard to deny its reality.

Who do you know yourself to be? Well, hopefully by now, you have heard the proposition that we are all children of the Creator. Along with this recognition comes the awareness of our Spiritual Heritage, which is embodied in the first three Rays. In this chapter, we want to focus on helping you raise your personal energetic vibration. This helps you to advance in your evolution by opening to a grander, greater expression of who you really are and what you are really able to become.

It is one thing to agree with a particular concept. It is quite another thing to actually own it. Let me give you an example. Many have heard or read the insight that we are spiritual beings that are experiencing a physical existence. But how many of us really own this insight? Think about all the implications of that statement and ask yourself if you own and practice all of what it entails. Many inferences can be drawn from that statement. Reincarnation is clearly part of that concept, along with creating your own reality, the Law of Attraction, and the loss of judgment. I could list a dozen more.

If you are anything like me, the transition from agreeing with something and owning it doesn't happen overnight. It is a gradual process. As you embrace one aspect of the insight, another presents itself for your ownership. And that is what this section is designed for. We can use the Seventh Ray as the Gateway into Awareness, whatever that awareness or insight may be. We will each move at our own personal speed, while staying within our own personal comfort zones.

This section provides a tool to help you experience your own individual spiritual spring. I have suggested throughout this entire book that you are more than you think yourself to be. And maybe you agree with that concept, but do you really own it? Is it real for you? It is OK if it isn't yet real. Work with this next aspect of the Seventh Ray, the Gateway into Awareness, and you will begin to experience that grander self. And if you do fully own the concept that you are more, then work with this section to experience an even fuller expression of what that means to you personally.

Awareness

Awareness is an ever-changing concept. If you think of what you knew yesterday morning and what you are aware of today, you will probably notice some differences. And the same is true for today and tomorrow. Every day each person's awareness expands. So awareness is simply the sum total of what you are aware of or know.

What do you call all the stuff you don't know? Recently, I was watching a video on YouTube about gravity and sacred geometry. Needless to say, I understood very little of it, especially the science of it. All of that is what I refer to as new awareness. Concepts were mentioned in the video that had meaning I was not aware of. I had heard of some of the other concepts before, but if you were to ask me to define what they were, I couldn't do it.

This next part gets a little tricky. I can say there are things that I know I don't know. There are terms that I am familiar with, but I don't really know what they mean. These are things I know I don't know, but I could spend the time and research them. Then there are things that I don't know that I don't know because I have never heard of them before. So I have just never considered some things before because I was totally unaware of them.

What does any of this have to do with the Seventh Ray? As the Gateway into Awareness, we use the Seventh Ray to help us open up our limiting beliefs about ourselves and our universe. No amount of reading is going to help you believe in your grandeur if you believe yourself to be weak, broken, or undeserving. And unfortunately, many institutions in our culture teach just that.

I mentioned earlier that the new Rays, the Rays of Soul Integration, are about expressing more of our greatness in this physical dimension. But before we can effectively work with those energies, we need to break up some logjams of personal awareness that have been created by our limiting beliefs.

Opening to new awareness requires change. It requires changes in beliefs. It requires changes in habituated patterns or habits. It requires changes in rituals that we may be involved with. As I mentioned earlier, rituals tend to promote the status quo. They tend to be restrictive. I know some will disagree with me about this, and that is fine. I'm not trying to convince anyone. I'm just suggesting that anything that might be considered a ritual be looked at and evaluated as to whether is it still helping you to move toward your goals.

When we work with the Seventh Ray as the Gateway into Awareness, we want to open doors, break through limiting barriers of beliefs, use our imaginations, and summon our courage to bravely go where we haven't gone before. We want to challenge our beliefs about ourselves and our personal abilities.

Here is a quote from the Team that explains a little bit more about using the Seventh Ray as the Gateway into Awareness.

> *The Violet Flame—call on the Violet Flame when you are ready, when those you work with are ready to acknowledge the resistance that they hold, when they are ready to accept what they are. You may find that it is hard to believe that most people, [we] would dare say most people on your planet, have yet to agree, to acknowledge their own perfection, their potential. They do not understand they do not have to suffer. They do not understand they do not have to live in difficulty.*
>
> *Jesus never desired to suffer, never desired for his people, all of mankind, to acknowledge any suffering from him. When you release this illusion, you open a door to releasing all discomfort, all pain. You open a new door to draw in more love, more light. We have an opportunity here in this life, not the next—in this life, in this experience—to be in unconditional love, to understand the joy, the simplicity, the harmony.*

When I have shared this quote from the Team in the past, I generally delete the sentence that mentions Jesus. Here in this section, I am leaving it in to emphasize that suffering is not what we came here to do. I think of difficulty and suffering as simply bad habits.

We came here to experience our true potential and to acknowledge our own perfection. We came here to experience unconditional love, to understand the joy of life, the simplicity, and the harmony. Sure, there is a big gap between what we have now and what our potential is. But unless we believe that we are capable of achieving these goals, we will never experience them. Self-imposed limits are just as formidable as real limits. The difference is that self-imposed limits can be removed.

In this next guided journey, we want to use the Seventh Ray to help us believe in our greatness. We have a Divine Heritage. We have tools given to us to create our lives however we see fit. All we need to do is create the vision of who we are and what we wish to create for ourselves without our previous self-imposed limitations. Get ready to open a few doorways to a new awareness of your perfection.

Guided Journey 5: THE SEVENTH RAY

You might want to consider working with Exercise 4 in the proceeding chapter before you complete this guided journey for the first time. Working with the image and the music of the Seventh Ray will certainly help you to strengthen your connection with it. Once you have done Guided Journey 5 a few times, then hopefully your connection has become stronger.

The purpose of this guided journey is to help you to envision some new possibilities for yourself. When you use the Seventh Ray to transmute the weightiness of past experience, it is very important to replace any limiting self-beliefs that you may have identified with new beliefs of who and what you are. Along with those new beliefs, it is important to visualize new personal goals and new heights of personal achievement.

An important aspect of this upcoming journey is envisioning yourself reaching personal goals that you may have never thought possible. Alternatively, you may refocus on prior goals that you have not yet been able to achieve, since you have now removed substantial roadblocks that prevented you from achieving those goals in the preceding chapters. Either approach works just fine.

As with all of the guided journeys, make sure you have about ten minutes of uninterrupted time in order to complete this experience. Find a comfortable place to sit. I suggest you read this guided journey all the way through first if you are going to do it on your own. Alternatively, you can go to my website, thetwelverays.com, where I have recorded it for you. I suggest you have paper and pen nearby, so at the end of this journey, you can write down any insights that may have come to you.

Let's begin this guided journey by focusing on your breathing. Take a gentle breath in and, as you do, imagine you are breathing in relaxing, fresh air. Take another gentle breath in and, with your exhale, imagine you are exhaling any stress or tension you may be feeling. Now take another gentle breath in, breathing in relaxation and breathing out any remaining stress or tension. Very good. Now continue with a gentle, rhythmic breathing pattern.

Envision a column of violet light descending from above your head. This is the energy of the Seventh Ray. Invite it to move through your entire body, starting at the top of your head and moving gently and slowly down through each of your seven chakras. Notice if you feel anything in those energy centers as you envision the violet light moving farther and farther down. Allow it to flow all the way down through your legs into the Earth. Envision it continuing to flow freely through your entire body.

Remember back to when you first learned to ride a bicycle. Someone probably helped you to get your balance, and then you took off on your own. You were understandably unsteady to begin with, but as you became more experienced with your bicycle, your confidence grew. At first, you probably kept to your own neighborhood. But soon you were able to ride to farther destinations, even outside of your neighborhood. Having a bike to ride gave you mobility and brought a certain sense of freedom to you.

Now envision yourself as a teenager learning how to drive a car. I'm sure there was a tangible sense of excitement in starting the engine for the first time and feeling the car begin to roll forward. It took a little bit longer to learn how to maneuver the car than it did to learn to ride the bike, but you soon became skillful enough to pass your driver's test and get your license. And with that driver's license, your world opened up even more. Your mobility extended beyond your neighborhood. You could now travel all around town with ease. You could even visit other towns if you wanted to. And as you got older you were able to take road trips, perhaps to other parts of the country.

Remember your first airplane ride. Remember the first time you flew to visit someone, or perhaps it was a vacation you took. You got on that big airplane full of excitement, not knowing what to expect. You strapped into your seat, and then the cabin lights were dimmed, and the plane rolled out to the runway. The plane got into position on the runway, and you heard the roar of the engines as the plane began to shake and lurch forward. It sped up, going faster and faster, and then it lifted off. Everything changed. You felt lighter. You were flying.

It climbed higher and higher, perhaps passing through some clouds, and then it broke through the clouds, and all you saw was blue sky. You saw yourself above the clouds for the first time. Remember what that felt like? Perhaps you were a little nervous. But the flight was smooth, and soon you landed at your destination, perhaps another part of the country or somewhere on the other side of the world. Now you had the freedom to travel all around the world.

As small children, we are not generally allowed to make too many of our own choices. As we get older, our desire to make our own decisions increases. Most teenagers desire more and more freedom to make their own decisions and organize their own resources to achieve their goals. Eventually, we strike out on our own as young adults, relying on our own talents and resources to get by.

You are capable of achieving whatever goals you have set for yourself. The question is, do you have the resources you need in order to achieve your goals? For whatever lifestyle you choose to live, do you have the right tools to help you achieve your objectives? Perhaps you don't have a clear idea of what your life goals are. That's OK. Remember that you can use the Sixth Ray to help you focus your intentions and create your life's objectives and goals.

Assuming that you do have some clarity about your goals, what mindset and tools did you use when you set your current life goals? Did you believe that you could only achieve very modest goals because you were only riding your bicycle? Did you think you could be a little more ambitious with your goals because you were driving your car? Perhaps you really felt empowered and created very ambitious goals for yourself because you felt you could use an airplane to achieve them?

What if I told you that you could set even more ambitious goals than your current ones simply by learning to fly your own airplane? What if you became the pilot of your own airplane? Think of how much more empowering that would be. You could set your own destinations and fly according to your own schedule whenever you wanted. Now, not everyone is ready to pilot their own airplane, and that is fine. But if you think this is something that you are ready for, then maybe you are asking yourself, "How do I learn how to fly my own airplane?"

How do you learn to expand your personal abilities beyond where they currently are right now? The first and perhaps most important step is to believe that you can. If you don't believe that a goal is real, how can you ever achieve it? The next step is to understand the path that will lead you to your goal of expanded personal abilities. Now, of course, this path is very individualized, but the good news is that other people have gone down similar paths. You can get some support from others who may have preceded you. They can help you to become aware of tools that will help you on your journey.

The Twelve Rays are such a tool. They help you to uncover limiting beliefs about yourself and replace them with expanded beliefs about who and what you really are. Your new beliefs help you to imagine creating a reality for yourself that may have seemed unreachable before.

If you are ready to learn to fly your own plane, if you are ready to create new goals for yourself that are based on expanded beliefs about who you are and what you are capable of, then you are ready to follow a new path of personal empowerment. Use the Twelve Rays and all the other tools that you have available to you to set those new goals.

In a moment, I will count from one to five and ask you to return to a full waking state. But before I do, ask yourself if you are ready to commit to leaving behind your limiting beliefs about yourself. Ask yourself if you are ready to move forward setting new goals for yourself that are based on your new beliefs about your true nature. Ask yourself if you are ready to use all the tools that you have available to you to help reach these new goals.

If you are ready to move on, then you are most likely ready to begin to work with the new, higher Rays. If you are uncertain or not yet ready to move forward, that is fine. Continue to work with the Rays of Experience until you find yourself ready to move to the next step.

I will now begin counting from one to five. One. Take a gentle breath in and, as you do, begin to allow your consciousness to return to your physical body. Two. Take another gentle breath in and gently begin to move your fingers and your toes. Three. As you take another gentle breath in, allow your consciousness to return more fully to your physical body, feeling your arms and your legs. Four. Feel your consciousness fully return to your physical body. Five. When you are ready, gently open your eyes and return to this place and this time feeling refreshed, relaxed, and better than you have felt all day.

Welcome back. Take this time to write down any insights that you received during this guided journey. Complete this guided journey as often as you like, until you feel you are ready to move on to the new Rays of Soul Integration.

"Your world is changing. [The Twelve Rays are] the energy that is available that makes this change, and it is the opening from higher wisdom that it has allowed this energy to flow. Your world is at a crucial point, and these energies are offered, as our wisdom is offered to you, for you to draw that part of it into your beingness, into Earth's beingness, to create as never before, to rise, to shine, to transcend your limits, to heal yourself. Are you not ready?"

– The Team

CHAPTER 10

You Are More

The Rays of Experience are yours to command. They are yours to use to help you experience what you came here to experience in this lifetime. They are energetic tools to help you be successful in achieving your goals. The more you use them, the greater your mastery of them becomes. You understand the depth and scope of these energies, and you become the master of your own personal energies. Just like an artist becomes master of the colors on her palette and uses color to give form and texture to her art, so you can use the energy of the Rays of Experience to create richness and fullness from your life experiences.

One of the exciting challenges of writing a book like this, one that is part informative and part experiential techniques, is that you have to write it for everyone. Everyone is going through a different personal journey. No two individuals are at the same place of awareness. So I strive to find common ground that as many as possible can relate to so that I can as clearly as possible share the information about the Twelve Rays. Here is an example. Everyone is in denial. And if you were one of the first to raise your hand and say, "But I'm not," then congratulations, you definitely are! Most of the time, we don't realize that we are in denial until it hits us right between the eyes.

I can be so confident in that statement because I know we come here with intentions that most of us could never complete in two lifetimes. We actually plan for numerous contingencies, so we can still find valuable experiences even when we take unforeseen paths. We have free will, and we can choose to take paths that lead us closer to our goals or paths that may lead us further away from our goals. It all depends on how much clarity we have about our intentions for this lifetime.

Sooner or later, most of us get to the point where we want to expand our understanding of who and what we are. We want to break out of the limits that we have accepted for ourselves up until now. When you get to this point, the new

Rays, Rays Eight through Twelve, are available to help you to integrate more of your whole self into this dimension.

Using these higher Rays, you can begin to anchor your Body of Light into your physical body here and now. Your Body of Light is the form you take on when you are done with your current physical life. It's the form you take when you cross over to the other side. We all have the opportunity to integrate more of our true selves, more of our Body of Light, into this physical vessel in our current lifetimes. And as we do, the New Awareness, which is the promise of the Eleventh and Twelfth Rays, becomes available to us. That gets me excited. I hope it has the same effect on you.

You are more than whatever you can imagine yourself to be beyond this dimension. How can I make such a confident statement about who you really are? Simple. The human mind was never intended to be able to comprehend the reality of your greatness. And that is OK. It doesn't serve you here in this dimension to have a full grasp of your real nature. You can have a better understanding of what you think you are, but your mind will never accurately portray the real you. And as I mentioned above, that is OK. Certain truths are meant to be transcendent to the human mind, at least for the foreseeable future.

Where does that leave us? A bigger you exists beyond this earthly experience. All that you experience within this current lifetime will be taken back with you to be integrated into that bigger you. Enjoy your adventures here on this planet in this dimension. Become a master of the Rays of Experience, and as you become that master, open up to the promise of the new Rays, the Rays of Soul Integration. Open up to the New Awareness that is waiting for us all. You can read more about the Rays of Soul Integration in my book, *The Reality of Your Greatness: A Personal Journey through the Twelve Rays*.

Always remember you are more than you think you are. And be sure to let your light shine!

ABOUT THE ARTISTS

Life can be seen as a journey. **Michael G. Love's** journey started in upstate New York. After graduating from college, he moved with his wife and young son to Bremen, Germany. They lived there for two years, thoroughly enjoying the culture, lifestyle, and hospitality of the German people. After returning home, Michael completed his master's degree and entered corporate America as a computer programmer. A new part of the journey had begun.

After over twenty years in corporate America, he founded a wellness center dedicated to alternative healing modalities. There he met Julie, the woman who was to change his life. She had messages for him from somewhere beyond this dimension. The story of that journey can be found in his book *The Reality of Your Greatness: A Personal Journey Through the Twelve Rays*. He followed that work with *The Twelve Rays Practical Applications*, a Rays of Aspect guide, a year later. He is delighted to share that he and Julie are still receiving messages from the Team. Find out about new book releases and events at MichaelGLove.com.

Keyboardist and composer **Richard Shulman** creates music intended to be a positive influence for himself, audiences, and society. Richard has recorded twenty-eight of his own albums as well as more than two dozen other recordings for which he has provided compositions, performances, and/or musical production. Trained in the classical and jazz fields, he has developed a heartfelt language in these genres while focusing a significant amount of his output on music for meditation, healing, and inspiration. Born and raised in Niagara Falls, New York, Richard currently lives in Asheville, North Carolina, and performs and records regionally, nationally, and internationally. For more information, visit RichHeartMusic.com.

As a professional intuitive artist, **Melinda Radcliffe's** work is a mixture of mediums and ranges from realism to abstract. She has clientele in the United States, Europe and China. For more information or to schedule a painting, please go to her website at melindaradcliffe.com.

Read about the Twelve Rays and the Reality of Your Greatness.

"If you are looking for a book that will help you understand life on a more intuitive and spiritual level, *The Reality of Your Greatness* will be on the of the best gifts you can give yourself and those you love."

– Amazon review

Listen to the accompanying music that has been described as:

"Powerful and completely Spiritual, this is a comprehensive body of work sent without doubt from the Divine to help connect to power, energy, and awareness, encompassing healing, love, meditation, and rebirth."

– Blue Wolf Review

Amazon Reviews for *The Reality of Your Greatness*

"Just finished this book. It is full of new concepts and insights on how to use energy to balance and improve ourselves. I already had an understanding that we live in an atomic world and energy is being used to transmit information. After all, wireless technology is common knowledge. But the author, Michael Love, talks about an energy containing a higher wisdom, that we can all tap into to help us move through challenges in our life and evolve ourselves with an understanding of a connection to a Greater Self. **It is thought provoking and has [piqued] my interest to know more.** He says we ARE more than we might imagine ourselves to be. (Wouldn't that be nice!)" – Judy

"Is there a purpose in this illusion we call life? In *The Reality of Your Greatness*, Mike Love is able to bring concepts that are difficult to grasp through guided mediations, music and the workbook style of this book. The feeling of being on our own is an illusion that we have chosen to experience, and with this knowledge we can begin to realize that we are MORE, which is enlightening and freeing. **This is a book that I have referred back to many times.**" – Melinda Radcliffe

"For those seeking a 'better' way to 'look' at life, *The Reality of Your Greatness* contains concise information and exercises to lead you to your higher state of being. Whether a beginner on this path, or, an advanced student, every Ray holds within it a practical goal that is entirely achievable. **The meditations are gifts to us all.** Well done!" – Marsha Cook

"The name for this book, *The Reality of Your Greatness*, says it all. As someone whose work is to help others recognize their own strength and abilities and to eliminate challenges preventing them from self-actualization and becoming their best self, I found this book to be filled with helpful information and practical application of the concepts presented on the energy of the Twelve Rays operating in all our lives. The presentation by the author of the energy of the Twelve Rays is both mind-blowing (it changes how you view the world as you read the book and use the powerful exercises and Ray infused music to feel the energy in your own way and at your own level) and reassuring. **The book and the accompanying musical CD take you on a journey of mind, body, and spirit I have not seen with any other book on the Twelve Rays.** If you are looking for a book that will help you understand life on a more intuitive and spiritual level, *The Reality of Your Greatness* will be one of the best gifts you can give yourself and those you love." – Dorothy Taylor, CLC, CH, Professional Astro-Life Coach, Astrologer, Hypnotist

"This book is a fantastic read. It was gifted to me, and I found it so inspiring and helpful, that I purchased one for my mother to have her own copy because I couldn't part with my own! For those who may be seeking more purpose in their lives, *The Reality of Your Greatness* contains insightful information and exercises that allow you to live your best life, and achieve your higher state of being. Whether you are a novice, or an advanced student on this path, the author relays the information in an approachable and achievable manner. **This book provided me with a lot of peace, hope, and a general better perspective on life, so a great and useful read for sure!**" – Brittany

What's Next?

Continue expanding your knowledge of the Twelve Rays' practical applications through online workshops.

Foundational Level Online Workshop
Rays One through Three

In this workshop, you will learn about the first three Rays, the Rays of Aspect. The Twelve Rays are a modern metaphor of spirituality for the digital age we are living in. I refer to the Rays of Aspect as our Divine Heritage. We all have the opportunity to embrace this heritage, and when we do, we bring the aspects of the Creator, Creative Thinking, Love, and Manifestation into our consciousness. These gifts become ours to command. Here are some of the practical techniques you will learn:
- Move beyond resistance to change.
- Reduce stress.
- Reduce the feeling of loneliness and replace it with connection.
- Open your heart to Love.
- Manifest whatever you choose.
- Successfully use the Law of Attraction.

Soul Integration Online Workshop
Rays Eight through Twelve

Work with the new Rays, which we refer to as the Rays of Soul Integration, to establish contact with your soul-level consciousness and begin to anchor the Body of Light into your current physical body here in this dimension. You will learn to:
- Bring inner clarity through your third eye using the Eighth Ray.
- Establish contact with your soul-level consciousness using the Ninth Ray.
- Establish contact with your Body of Light using the Ninth Ray.
- Begin to anchor your Body of Light into your physical structure.
- Connect with and direct Spiritual Microtrons (smallest units of energy).
- Begin to connect with the New Awareness.

Find more information about all the online workshops at thetwelverays.com

www.ingramcontent.com/pod-product-compliance
Lightning Source LLC
Chambersburg PA
CBHW050754110526
44592CB00003B/63